Corked & Forked

Corked & Forked

Four Seasons of Eats & Drinks

by Keith Wallace

RUNNING PRESS
PHILADELPHIA · LONDON

Books published by Running Press are available at special dis-
counts for bulk purchases in the United States by corporations,
institutions, and other organizations. For more information,
please contact the Special Markets Department at the Perseus
Books Group, 2300 Chestnut Street, Suite 200, Philadelphia, PA
19103, or call (800) 810-4145, ext. 5000, or e-mail special.mar-
kets@perseusbooks.com.

ISBN 978-0-7624-3982-9
Library of Congress Control Number: 2010941542

E-book ISBN 978-0-7624-4365-9

9   8   7   6   5   4   3   2   1
Digit on the right indicates the number of this printing

Photography by Steve Legato
    Page 67: iStock © MadCircles

Design by Joshua McDonnell
Edited by Kristen Green Wiewora
Typography: Archer, Vertrina, and Whitney

Running Press Book Publishers
2300 Chestnut Street
Philadelphia, PA 19103-4371

Visit us on the web!
www.runningpress.com

To Alana

table of contents

ACKNOWLEDGMENTS

Although every word is mine, I didn't write this book alone.

First and foremost, I must thank Alana Zerbe. In my mind, she is the uncredited co-author of this book. Alana somehow managed to translate my grease-stained notes into exceptionally vivid recipes, coax my occasionally chaotic ideas into manageable prose, and generally keep me on the straight and narrow.

Four others stand out as being instrumental in turning a great idea into an actual book. First is Josh McDonnell, who championed *Corked & Forked* from the very beginning. The second is Brian Freedman, who inspired me to begin writing. The third is Joy Manning, who risked our longstanding friendship by offering her frank opinion of my first draft. Finally, there is my editor Kristen Green Wiewora, who was my lifeline throughout the publishing process.

There are so many more who helped in ways big and small. There are the brave souls who attended my monthly Corked & Forked cooking classes; my staff at the Wine School of Philadelphia who kept the place running smoothly while I wrote; and my friends whom I callously used as guinea pigs for some of my more extreme culinary ideas.

There are two others I want to acknowledge. Originally, their names were listed at the top of this page, but it was pointed out that they really didn't help with the book at all. In fact, they aren't even human: they are my dogs, Rosie and Coco. What can I say? I love them to bits.

INTRODUCTION

E ating and drinking came first. Before we became lawyers or journalists or architects, we were chefs and brewers and winemakers. Every animal eats and drinks, but we prepare meals, and we always have. Way back in some prehistoric cave, our ancestors were roasting meat, brewing grain, and fermenting fruits to nourish the clan.

Suppertime is literally in our DNA.

In our modern world, the magic of a perfect food and beverage pairing is one of the first lessons we learn. It arrives with the first bite of a freshly baked chocolate chip cookie followed by a sip of milk. The flavors sparkle and flicker, then hit something gooey and primal in an ancient corner of the brain. Immediately we think: I want more of that. I MUST HAVE MORE!

The perfect pairing is an irresistible force that begins with little fingers and sippy cups and eventually graduates to forks and corks. While most meals demand beverages a bit more sophisticated than 2% milk, great pairings don't have to be complex: often they are as simple as serving Champagne with potato chips.

Corked & Forked isn't meant to be your typical entertainment guide. The goal is to create great meals in the simplest of ways. The recipes are designed to take advantage of everything a given season has to offer, and the menus work together seamlessly. The dishes are not hard to prepare; most are inspired by the stripped-down recipes I used as a professional chef. Even better, almost all the ingredients are easily found at a local grocery.

The book isn't strictly about cooking either: it's about experiencing gustatory epiphanies, preferably with the most important people in your life. That means popping open a bottle or two or twenty. For each dish in this book, I offer a selection of pairings that will throw open the door to the full potential of a meal. This allows you to understand the keys to pairing, and will lay the foundation for discovering lip-smacking synchronicities of your own. To paraphrase Alexis Lichine, if you want to learn about wine or beer or cocktails, grab a corkscrew and use it.

Above all, this book is about experimentation. It might be very pretty, but it was not made to sit politely on a coffee table. It will have a fit if you try to put it on a dusty shelf with other cookbooks. It wants to share an adventure with you. There should be stains on at least a dozen of its pages; illegible notes scrawled in the margins; and a scattering of torn corners.

After all, *Corked & Forked* is dedicated to a singular and primal act: breaking bread with your clan. Enjoy.

Keith Wallace

SUMMER

SUMMERTIME IS ALL ABOUT FLASH: The glittering flash of a white sail over blue water, the spicy flash of a jalapeño pepper in a crisp salad, the reflected flash of a smile in the rear-view mirror. The days are long and languid, promising glittering moments of white-hot laughter and half-remembered dalliances.

Of course, there will be unhappy moments of either scorching heat or torrential rains. But most days will be just sunshine and blue sky and dinner plans. IT'S TIME TO LIVE, EAT, AND DRINK FOR THE MOMENT. Could there be anything better?

Days on end of pure sunshine turn us all into little kids. It's nearly impossible to be taken seriously when wearing flip flops and eating seafood from a bucket. And that's okay, because one of the greatest gifts of summer is the playfulness of its food. Bright colors pop off the dinner plate. FLAVORS SIZZLE AND SING ON THE TONGUE. Farmstands overflow with bright reds and shiny greens. An instantaneous high is delivered just by sinking your teeth into fruits and vegetables that are dripping with ripeness.

With such bounty, cooking becomes quite simple. In my recipes I KEEP FLAVORS CLEAN, LIGHT, AND FULL OF ZEST. Hot peppers, dramatic spices, and brilliant citruses all make frequent appearances in these summer chapters. And we can do more with less during this season since locally grown produce lends so much more flavor than the typical supermarket fare.

Summer cooking should also minimize use of the kitchen stove. With that in mind, these recipes will involve a lot of pickling, curing, and outdoor grilling. Don't sweat it if you are without one of those gleaming new barbeques. EVERY GRILLED RECIPE IN THIS BOOK WAS CREATED ON A $25 GRILL PURCHASED AT A FLEA MARKET.

THE BURGER

Where do you begin a book on cooking, eating, and drinking? I'm taking a chance that the burger—one of the most versatile and classic of summer dishes—is as good as it gets. Who doesn't love a burger? Americans eat ten billion of 'em every year. And I am not talking about the hamburger, because just-hamburgers went out of fashion a long time ago. Buffalo, rabbit, salmon, mushroom, and even fava beans have taken the humble patty to new heights.

The truth is that anyone can make a great burger. There are only a few essentials that you will need. The first is a spot of ground outside big enough to drop a grill, preferably a charcoal-fired one. The second is time: give yourself a twenty-four hour head start since we will be making almost everything from scratch.

Let's talk about the beef burger first. No matter how done you like your meat, the end result should be moist but not greasy, meaty but not steaky. It also should be easy to eat with one hand, allowing you to hold your beverage in the other. But the burger should never be an antiseptic undertaking. Each bite should leave the fingers respectfully messy—enough to indulge your inner child in some summer fun without looking like you just changed the oil on a Chevy Impala.

The veggie burger should have the same characteristics, replacing the meaty flavor with other earthy and vaguely sinful tastes. Deeply intense mushrooms like portabella or porcini infused with smoke and oil is the key to great flavor for this burger. In this chapter I invite you to devote some time to making the veggie burger its meaty-best. Trust me, the world just might be a better place.

While there is a trend to use English muffins, challah bread, or glazed donuts for the bun, the best match for any patty is the good old white bread bun from the supermarket. It provides the perfect blank slate on which to drop sharp and exotic bursts of flavor.

The condiments must be well thought out, too. The richness of the burger needs to be balanced with the sweetness of pickle, the spiciness of mustard, and the sharpness of relish. Here's the really beautiful and crazy thing about these all-American condiments: they are a millennium older than our country and hail from various points along the Asian continent. My modern update of these ancient recipes will create our secret sauce for the ultimate burger.

Early Summer Salad with Flowers

A simple salad is the best accompaniment for this meal. The edible flowers add visual appeal and a bit of peppery spice. Both nasturtiums and orchids are in season right now, but if you can't find any, just double up on the tomatoes. The one essential ingredient is high-quality vinegar; this recipe calls for 6-year balsamic.

SERVES 4 TO 6

2 CUPS EDIBLE FLOWERS, DIVIDED
2 CUPS CHERRY TOMATOES, QUARTERED
2 TABLESPOONS EXTRA-VIRGIN OLIVE OIL
2 TABLESPOONS ROASTED WALNUT OIL
2 TEASPOONS KOSHER SALT
4 TEASPOONS 6-YEAR BALSAMIC VINEGAR

Toss one cup of the flowers together with the tomatoes in a large bowl. Add the olive oil, walnut oil, salt, and balsamic vinegar, coating the salad thoroughly. Divide and serve, using the remaining flowers as garnish.

Vegetabalarian Burger

When prepared properly, a simple portabella mushroom cap can make a fantastic burger. This one boasts a toothsome firmness, rich smoky flavors, and just the right amount of grease.

SERVES 4

4 LARGE PORTABELLA MUSHROOM CAPS
4 TEASPOONS ROASTED WALNUT OIL
4 TEASPOONS EXTRA-VIRGIN OLIVE OIL
2 TEASPOONS KOSHER SALT
2 TEASPOONS FRESHLY GROUND BLACK PEPPER
4 HAMBURGER BUNS
¼ CUP HOMEMADE KETCHUP (PAGE 20), MORE OR LESS TO TASTE
¼ CUP ROASTED SHALLOT RELISH (PAGE 21), MORE OR LESS TO TASTE

Preheat the grill to a high heat.

Place the mushrooms on a sheet tray, gills-side up. Drizzle each mushroom with 1 teaspoon of the walnut oil. Flip them over and drizzle the tops with 1 teaspoon of the olive oil.

Grill the mushrooms, gill-side down, for 5 minutes. Flip and continue to grill for another 5 minutes, or until the caps have dark grill marks. Sprinkle each mushroom with ½ teaspoon of salt and ½ teaspoon of pepper. Place in a bun and dress with the Homemade Ketchup (page 20) and the Roasted Shallot Relish (page 21). Serve immediately.

"Wagyū-ish" Burgers

Rendered fat is the key to this recipe; we will use it to mimic the flavor of wagyū beef, also known as Kobe, which has a very high fat content. Make sure to start cooking the bacon about two hours before dinner (or even the night before) to ensure that you will have enough on hand.

SERVES 4 TO 6

8 OUNCES BACON

½ CUP ROASTED WALNUT OIL, IF NEEDED

1 POUND GROUND ANGUS BEEF, 80% LEAN

¼ POUND SHARP PROVOLONE, THINLY SLICED

6 HAMBURGER BUNS

¼ CUP HOMEMADE KETCHUP (PAGE 20), MORE OR LESS
   TO TASTE

¼ CUP ROASTED SHALLOT RELISH (PAGE 21), MORE OR
   LESS TO TASTE

Preheat the oven to 350°F. Lay out the slices of bacon on a sheet tray, ¼-inch apart, and roast for 25 minutes, or until the bacon is crispy. Drain the fat from the bacon into a glass measuring cup. If you have less than ½ cup of fat after roasting, then add the roasted walnut oil to supplement, resulting in ½ cup of fat. If you have more than ½ cup of rendered fat, discard the extra. Allow the bacon and the fat to cool for 30 minutes at room temperature.

Preheat the grill to a medium-high heat.

In a large metal bowl, pour out the fat and add the ground beef. Mix together until the oil has been completely absorbed. Form the ground beef into six patties, about 1¼-inches thick.

Grill the beef for 5 minutes, or until the meat pulls away from the grill grate. Flip the burgers, top with the sliced provolone, and grill for about 4 more minutes for a rare burger, and 7 minutes for a medium burger. Place in a bun and dress with one tablespoon each of the Homemade Ketchup (page 20) and the Roasted Shallot Relish (page 21). Serve immediately.

Homemade Ketchup

Ketchup is one of those foods with a longer history than most countries. The sauce actually dates back to ancient China where one of the ingredients was fermented fish. While that may sound really unappetizing, the combonation did what modern ketchup still does: adds an umami richness to any dish. This sauce will store in the refrigerator for up to three weeks.

MAKES 2½ CUPS

- 1 TABLESPOON EXTRA-VIRGIN OLIVE OIL
- 1 SPANISH ONION (ABOUT 1 CUP), DICED
- 4 CLOVES GARLIC, MINCED
- 1½ TEASPOONS KOSHER SALT
- 2 WHOLE CLOVES
- 1 BAY LEAF
- ¼ TEASPOON GROUND CINNAMON
- 1 TABLESPOON SWEET PAPRIKA
- ¼ TEASPOON CELERY SEEDS
- ¼ TEASPOON RED CHILE FLAKES
- 2 TEASPOONS CAYENNE PEPPER
- ¼ TEASPOON GROUND ALLSPICE
- ¼ TEASPOON GROUND CORIANDER
- 1 TEASPOON FRESHLY GROUND BLACK PEPPER
- ½ CUP WHITE VINEGAR
- ½ CUP DARK BROWN SUGAR
- 1 (32-OUNCE) CAN WHOLE TOMATOES, IN JUICE
- 2 TABLESPOONS SOY SAUCE

Place a 4-quart sauté pan over medium-high heat. Add the oil, onion, garlic, and salt. Once the onions caramelize, after about 3 minutes, add the herbs and spices. Cook for 3 minutes, until the spices start to darken. Add the vinegar, sugar, tomatoes, and soy sauce. Continue to cook for 45 minutes over medium-high heat, stirring every 5 minutes, until the tomatoes break down completely and the ketchup is reduced by one-third. Make sure to scrape the bottom of the pan as you stir. The result should be thick as pudding.

Remove the bay leaves, then purée the sauce in a food processor or a blender until smooth. Return to the saucepan and cook over medium-low heat. Let simmer for 30 minutes, stirring every 3 minutes.

Turn off the heat, remove the sauce from the burner, and let cool for 1 hour. Transfer to a plastic squeeze bottle or other serving container. Cover with a tight-fitting lid or plastic wrap and refrigerate.

Roasted Shallot Relish

Pickles, relish, and mustard are essential condiments, too. I adapted this Indo-Pakistani chutney to be a bridge to all those flavors. It's a pickled relish with mustard, and spicy! Slathered onto a grilled burger, this relish adds a remarkable depth and balance to every bite. The intense flavors come from the unique trick of poaching whole shallots in a shallot purée.

MAKES 2 CUPS

1 POUND SHALLOTS, PEELED AND DIVIDED

¼ CUP ROASTED SESAME SEED OIL

1½ TEASPOONS MUSTARD SEEDS

1 TEASPOON KOSHER SALT

2 TEASPOONS LEMON JUICE, FRESHLY SQUEEZED

2 BAY LEAVES

4 TEASPOONS CAYENNE

¼ TEASPOON ONION POWDER

¼ TEASPOON CURRY POWDER

2 TEASPOONS DARK BROWN SUGAR

Take 4 ounces of the shallots, chop them roughly, and purée in a food processor or blender to make a paste. In a sauté pan over medium heat, heat the sesame oil, then add the mustard seeds. When the seeds start to sputter in the oil, add the remaining whole shallots, the shallot paste, and the salt. Stir every 3 to 4 minutes. When not stirring, keep the pan covered, cooking for 10 to 15 minutes, or until the shallots are slightly browned.

Add the lemon juice, bay leaves, cayenne, onion powder, curry powder, and sugar, along with ½ cup of water. Cook over medium heat, stirring every 2 minutes for 10 minutes, or until the sauce has thickened to a paste. Remove from the heat and let cool to room temperature.

Once cool, remove the whole shallots and slice them into small rounds, then add them back to the sauce. Refrigerate until ready to serve. The relish will keep in the refrigerator for up to two weeks.

Cantaloupe & Gin Popsicle

The combination of cantaloupe, cucumber, and gin offers up surprisingly sophisticated flavors that will delight and amuse your guests. For the mold, you can use a traditional 4-ounce popsicle mold or even small paper cups.

SERVES 6

½ MEDIUM CANTALOUPE (ABOUT 3 CUPS), RIND REMOVED, SEEDED AND ROUGHLY CHOPPED

½ SEEDLESS CUCUMBER, PEELED AND ROUGHLY CHOPPED (CAN SUBSTITUTE ½ ENGLISH CUCUMBER, HALVED LENGTHWISE, SEEDS SCRAPED OUT)

2 TABLESPOONS PREMIUM-QUALITY GIN

½ CUP SUGAR (OPTIONAL)

Purée the cantaloupe, cucumber, and gin in a blender until smooth. Taste, and add sugar if desired. Fill the popsicle molds with the mixture. Place in the freezer and wait patiently for six hours for the popsicles to freeze. Remove from the mold, running water over the outside if necessary, and serve.

BEVERAGE PAIRINGS

Sazerac

The first and most obvious pairing for a burger is beer. If you can find it, grab a six-pack of California common, also known as steam beer. This is a uniquely California-style lager dating back to the nineteenth century when brewers couldn't rely on modern inventions like refrigeration. This beer is heavier than most lagers and stands up to burgers like it was going into battle. Plus, its malty flavors and wild slap of hops balance out the sweetness of the ketchup.

For red wines, the uber-American choice is an old vine red Zinfandel from the Mendocino Ridge wine region of Northern California. Wines in this area are still made from vines planted during the California Gold Rush. And they are as macho as their history: These full-throttle fruit bombs will get you buzzed first and ask questions later.

For the cocktail, we have to go with the Sazerac, which is arguably both the first and greatest American cocktail. The recipe has evolved over the centuries, but this is the closest you'll come to the original. Do yourself a favor and use rye whiskey and not bourbon, which is a bit too smooth for this drink.

SERVES 1

ICE CUBES
¼ TEASPOON GRANULATED SUGAR
1½ OUNCES RYE WHISKEY
2 DASHES (¼ TEASPOON) PEYCHAUD BITTERS
SPLASH (½ TEASPOON) ABSINTHE
TWIST OF LEMON PEEL

Fill an old fashioned glass or short tumbler with ice. Put the sugar in a second glass of the same type. Add the rye, the bitters, and a few cubes of ice, and stir. Discard the ice from the first glass, and pour in the absinthe. Turn the glass around in your hands to coat the sides with the absinthe, then pour out the excess. Strain the rye mixture into the absinthe-coated glass. Twist and squeeze a lemon peel over the drink. Rub the rim of the glass with the peel, discarding it when finished, and serve.

TWENTIES-ERA SUMMER PICNIC

For centuries, the combination of blankets, baskets, and blue sky has meant only one thing: it's time to collect your friends and head to your favorite patch of countryside. We think of the picnic as a carefree day of uncomplicated pleasures, but until the roaring twenties, everything was a bit more complicated.

Just a few years earlier, the English-speaking world was stuck in the Victorian era. Picnics were still about hunting parties, kidney pie, and possibly a game of blind man's bluff. There were entire books on proper picnic etiquette. Then, poof! it was the modern world of Maxfield Parrish, F. Scott Fitzgerald, the nineteenth amendment—and jarred mayonnaise.

Modernism and mayo hit the picnic at the same time, and the result was the trifecta of deviled eggs, chicken salad sandwiches, and potato salad that still reigns supreme today. Suddenly, picnics weren't about games of croquet and cucumber sandwiches. They were about tossing a quick meal together and jumping in your Packard Twin Six for an afternoon drive, and perhaps dropping into a speakeasy for a quick martini.

When you think about it, mayo is an odd addition to outdoor eating: Who in their right mind thought a sandwich with raw egg dressing was the perfect thing to serve in the summer heat? In any event, that brave soul became the pioneer of modern American picnics.

For this chapter, I reached back to some vintage twenties-era cookbooks for inspiration. I didn't recreate these dishes as much as resurrect some forgotten flourishes and adapted them to the modern palate. They have a familiar and easy quality that is key to a picnic, with just the right amount of pizzazz to keep them interesting. And I kept the mayo.

Smoke-Dusted Deviled Eggs

A favorite of Thomas Jefferson. Honestly, how many times can you say that about a food? In this preparation, I add a drop of truffle oil and a dusting of smoked paprika. These elements make the yolk richer and earthier. Just be careful not to use too much since both ingredients are dangerously potent.

SERVES 4 TO 6

6 EGGS

3 TEASPOONS FINE SALT, DIVIDED

½ CUP MAYONNAISE

1 TEASPOON TRUFFLE OIL

TWO PINCHES (⅛ TEASPOON) SMOKED PAPRIKA, DIVIDED

1 MINCED TABLESPOON CHIVES

To make the hard-cooked eggs, gently place the eggs side-by-side in a medium-sized saucepan. Cover with cold water, about 1 inch over the top of the eggs, and 1 teaspoon of salt. Bring to a boil over high heat. Boil rapidly for 1 minute before covering the pan and turning off the heat. Let the eggs rest in the water bath for 15 minutes before shocking with cold water to stop the cooking process. Peel the eggs.

Cut the hard-cooked eggs in half lengthwise. Remove the yolks and place them in a mixing bowl. Mash the yolks with the back of a fork until smooth. Add the mayonnaise, truffle oil, a pinch of paprika, and the remaining salt. Blend thoroughly.

Lay out the cooked egg whites and sprinkle with the remaining smoked paprika. With a small spoon, fill the eggs' yolk cavity with the yolk mixture. Sprinkle a small amount of the chives over the yolk. Keep refrigerated until ready to serve.

Spanish Chicken Salad

This salad's balance of sweet and savory elements, as well as its slightly exotic character, makes it perfect for any occasion. This dish can be made one day in advance.

SERVES 6

¼ TEASPOON FINE SALT

¼ TEASPOON FRESHLY GROUND BLACK PEPPER

¼ CUP ALL-PURPOSE FLOUR

4 CHICKEN BREAST HALVES, (ABOUT 1 POUND) FAT REMOVED, CUT INTO ½-INCH CUBES

3 TABLESPOONS EXTRA-VIRGIN OLIVE OIL, DIVIDED

1 TABLESPOON DICED SHALLOTS

2 TABLESPOONS SHERRY VINEGAR

¼ CUP MAYONNAISE

1 FENNEL BULB, DICED

2 TABLESPOONS SLICED, TOASTED ALMONDS

1 LARGE ZUCCHINI (8 OUNCES), DICED

2 ROASTED RED PEPPERS (8 OUNCES), DICED

In a large bowl, mix the salt, pepper, and flour. Add the chicken and toss, making sure to evenly coat the meat.

Preheat a large sauté pan over medium-high heat for about 2 minutes. Add 2 tablespoons of olive oil, then add the chicken. Make sure to not crowd the pan (you may have to cook the chicken in batches). Wait until the chicken cubes are golden-brown, about 3 minutes, before turning them over. Flip and cook for another 3 minutes, or until completely cooked. Remove from the pan when done. Drain the chicken cubes on a paper towel. Set aside.

Add 1 tablespoon of olive oil and the shallots to the pan. Let them cook until they turn translucent, about 1 to 2 minutes. Add ½ cup of water and the vinegar to the pan, and scrape the bottom to make sure the drippings from the chicken dissolve into the sauce. Once the sauce comes to a boil, about 2 minutes, remove pan from heat. In another large stainless steel bowl, add the chicken, mayonnaise, fennel, almonds, zucchini, and peppers. Mix the ingredients thoroughly. Add the sauce to the bowl, once again mixing completely. Let the salad rest in the refrigerator until cool. Serve.

Potato & Prosciutto Salad

This is potato salad with fancy mustard and ham! It's trashy and classy at the same time, and somehow that just makes it feel oh so right. The salad is best if the potato pieces are uniform in size. Also, feel free to use the cheapest prosciutto you can find. There is no reason to use the expensive stuff in this dish. The salad can be made up to six hours before serving.

SERVES 4 TO 6

¼ CUP FINE SALT

1½ POUNDS NEW POTATOES (ABOUT 4½ CUPS), QUARTERED

1 CUP MAYONNAISE

1 SHALLOT, MINCED

1 TEASPOON DIJON MUSTARD

2 TEASPOONS KOSHER SALT

1 TEASPOON FRESHLY GROUND BLACK PEPPER

2 GARLIC CLOVES, MINCED

6 SLICES PROSCIUTTO (ABOUT 2 OUNCES), THINLY SLICED

2 TEASPOONS ITALIAN PARSLEY, CHOPPED

1 BUNCH ARUGULA (ABOUT 1½ CUPS), TORN INTO BITE-SIZED PIECES

In a large sauté pan over high heat, boil 1 gallon of water with the salt. Carefully add the potatoes, and bring the water back up to boil for 2 minutes. Reduce to medium heat and simmer for about 10 minutes, or until the potatoes turn tender. Drain the potatoes and let cool to room temperature.

To make the dressing, whisk the mayonnaise, shallots, mustard, salt, pepper, and garlic in a large bowl. Once blended, add the prosciutto, parsley, and potatoes. Toss gently with the arugula and serve.

Innocent Cupcakes with Evil Frosting

This recipe is the one and only time I will use a product name in my cookbook. The reason is because there isn't anything else quite like Marshmallow Fluff. This was invented near where I grew up, and I still have a fondness for the goopy stuff. This easy sponge cake is low in fat but the frosting sure as hell isn't! If you have an electric mixer, you should definitely use it for creaming the frosting.

MAKES 1 DOZEN

Cupcakes
6 LARGE EGGS, SEPARATED
¼ TEASPOON CREAM OF TARTAR
1 CUP GRANULATED SUGAR
1 CUP CAKE FLOUR
¼ TEASPOON FINE SALT
1 TEASPOON FRESHLY SQUEEZED LEMON JUICE
¼ TEASPOON VANILLA EXTRACT

Frosting
¾ CUP LARD
8 OUNCES MARSHMALLOW FLUFF
½ TEASPOON VANILLA EXTRACT
½ CUP CONFECTIONERS' SUGAR

Preheat the oven to 325°F. Fill a cupcake pan with paper liners and set aside. Place two large mixing bowls in the freezer for 10 minutes.

For the cupcakes: In one of the chilled bowls, add the egg whites and beat until they are just slightly frothy. Add the cream of tartar and continue beating the egg whites until stiff peaks form, about 2 minutes. Set aside.

In the second chilled bowl, beat the egg yolks until they become thick and lemon-colored, about 3 minutes. Add the sugar gradually, mixing after each addition, and mix until well blended. Using a spatula, stir the flour and the salt into the egg yolks, one-third at a time, making sure to incorporate the flour completely.

Add the lemon juice and the vanilla extract to the egg yolk batter. Fold the batter into the beaten egg whites with a spatula.

Spoon the batter into the cupcake liners and bake for 20 to 25 minutes, or until a toothpick inserted into the center of a cupcake comes out clean.

Cool the cupcakes completely in their pans before removing them and adding the frosting.

For the frosting: Whip the lard with an electric mixer until it doubles in volume, about 4 minutes. Stir in the Marshmallow Fluff and the vanilla and continue to whip until it becomes light and fluffy, about 7 minutes. Slowly add the confectioners' sugar and continue to beat. When thoroughly blended, scoop the frosting into a pastry bag fitted with a wide tip or into a large plastic resealable bag with one corner cut off. Pipe the frosting onto the top of the cupcakes. Serve.

BEVERAGE PAIRINGS

Picnic drinks are a category unto themselves. It's a hot summer day and your guests are parched, so the finer points of beverage pairings are probably going to be lost as they knock back cold drinks from plastic cups. Pairings here are more about being appropriate for the occasion and the weather than the actual dishes being served.

For beer, an ice-cold Scottish pale ale (also known as an ESB or Extra Special Bitter) is the clear winner. It is light and malty without a noticeably hoppy bite. This is basically Gatorade for foodies.

For wine, it has to be either white or pink. A white Vinho Verde from Portugal is like a splash of ice-cold water on the face. For pink, you could go with a dry rosé from the Rhône Valley in France. However, if you want to wave your freak flag and have a secret passion for white Zinfandel, now is the time to pop open a bottle.

Caipirinha

For an outdoor cocktail most folks go for a mojito, but my picnic favorite is the caipirinha. The essential ingredient in this drink is cachaça, which is a Brazilian spirit similar to rum. You can substitute rum, but before you do, roll over to your local liquor store and see if they carry cachaça. It's worth the extra effort.

SERVES 1

1 LIME, QUARTERED
1 TABLESPOON GRANULATED SUGAR
2½ OUNCES CACHAÇA
1 CUP ICE CUBES

In an old fashioned glass or small tumbler, squeeze and drop in 2 quarters of a lime. Add the sugar and muddle the mixture with a spoon. Pour in 2½ ounces of the cachaça and 1 cup of ice. Use the remaining lime as garnish or for your next drink. Stir well and serve immediately.

GRILLING WITH FRIENDS

You should fear my grilling skills: I spent years working the grill in restaurants up and down the East Coast. By the time I retired my chef's jacket, I was a grill master, second to none. That distinction stayed intact for many a year, until the day I met Dani and discovered that I didn't know a thing.

Fast forward a decade to my first stint as a winemaker. Dani was my newest employee and we were gearing up for bottling. She earned my respect pretty quickly hauling cases and equipment like a cellar rat three times her size. When the winery staff had a few days off around the Fourth of July, Dani invited all of us to her place for a barbecue. Nearly the entire crew showed up at her door.

The sight of a dozen disheveled men didn't faze her in the least. She lit up her old rusty grill and within a half hour was grilling away. Throughout the whole evening, Dani never broke a sweat. She kept smoking a cigarette, laughing, and telling dirty jokes while occasionally serving up a perfectly cooked bison burger or blood sausage. It was easily one of the best meals I had ever had.

Reflecting back, I now see that my friend's grill mastery was based on three pillars: an adamant will to have fun; a certain carnivorous delight in cooking meat; and a general fearlessness bordering on recklessness. It's a simple recipe for greatness in cooking, and yes, so much harder to master than it sounds. I have found that by having everything prepped ahead of time—leaving just a few things ready to toss on the grill—is the best way to emulate Dani's skills. Oh, and a drink beforehand works wonders, too.

Grilled Watermelon Salad

A uniquely summery salad that is visually stunning and delicious. The sweetness of the watermelon counteracts the briny quality of the feta and olives. For the finish, the spinach is tossed in the watermelon marinade, giving it a refreshing vinaigrette.

SERVES 8

¼ CUP EXTRA-VIRGIN OLIVE OIL

2 TEASPOONS KOSHER SALT

½ TEASPOON FRESHLY GROUND BLACK PEPPER

1 SMALL SEEDLESS WATERMELON (ABOUT 5 POUNDS), CUT INTO 8 SLICES

1 POUND BABY SPINACH (ABOUT 6 CUPS)

1 CUP CRUMBLED FETA CHEESE

¾ CUP GREEN OLIVES (ABOUT 16), PITTED AND DICED

Preheat the grill. Remove the watermelon rind and discard. In a large bowl, add the olive oil, salt, and pepper. Toss the watermelon slices into the seasoned olive oil, coating thoroughly.

Grill the watermelon for 2 minutes on each side, or until dark grill marks form on the flesh.

Toss the spinach leaves into the reserved marinade.

To assemble, plate the watermelon and greens side by side on individual plates. Sprinkle each grilled watermelon slice with the feta cheese and at least two olives, and serve immediately.

Brined and Thymed Pork

Curing pork uses pretty much the same process as making a fresh ham, except that it will take five full days to brine properly. During this process, it is essential that the pork shoulder become completely submerged in the brine. If you do not have a large enough container, you can use your refrigerator's vegetable drawer; just make sure to clean it thoroughly afterward.

SERVES 6

1 CUP KOSHER SALT

¾ CUP GRANULATED SUGAR

2 BAY LEAVES

5 WHOLE BLACK PEPPERCORNS

1 TABLESPOON DRIED THYME

1 TABLESPOON DRIED MARJORAM

5 GARLIC CLOVES, PEELED

3 POUNDS BONELESS PORK SHOULDER

Pour 2½ gallons of cold water into a large, nonreactive container that can hold the brine. Stir in the salt and sugar. Slightly crush the bay leaves, peppercorns, thyme, and marjoram in your hand, and add these herbs, along with the garlic, to the container. Add the pork and submerge it in the brine. Place a heavy plate on top of the shoulder to keep the meat completely submerged. Refrigerate for 5 to 8 days.

Remove the pork from the brine and pat dry. Preheat the grill on medium heat.

Grill the pork shoulder over a medium fire for about 1 hour, turning every 15 minutes, until the internal temperature reaches 160°F. Slice into thin steaks, about ¼-inch thick, and serve.

Grilled Vegetable Kebabs

I freaking love grilled zucchini. If I were going to write a vegetarian cookbook it would probably just have this recipe on every page. The most important thing is to make sure that the veggies are uniform in size; otherwise some of the pieces won't touch the grate. Serve the kebabs as an entrée or alongside the Brined and Thymed Pork (page 36).

SERVES 4 TO 6

½ CUP EXTRA-VIRGIN OLIVE OIL

1 TABLESPOON KOSHER SALT

1 TEASPOON FRESHLY GROUND BLACK PEPPER

1 ZUCCHINI, SLICED INTO 1-INCH-THICK RINGS

1 PINT CHERRY TOMATOES (ABOUT 2 CUPS)

8 OUNCES CRIMINI MUSHROOMS (ABOUT 1 CUP), OR
    BUTTON MUSHROOMS

3 SHALLOTS, PEELED AND QUARTERED

If using wooden skewers, soak in water for 30 minutes.

In a large mixing bowl, blend the oil, salt, and pepper. Add the zucchini, tomatoes, mushrooms, and shallots and toss. Thread the vegetables onto skewers, about 5 per skewer. Grill for 8 minutes, turning over every 2 to 3 minutes, until the shallots become caramelized and soft. Remove from the grill and let cool before serving.

Grilled Apple and Walnut Charoset

Charoset is an ancient Jewish dessert of wine, honey, and fruit from the Middle East. Mine is a modern version using tawny port. No matter how you update it, the combination of honey, nuts, and apples is still one of the best summertime desserts.

SERVES 4 TO 6

½ STICK (4 TABLESPOONS) UNSALTED BUTTER

2 RED APPLES, PEELED, CORED, AND HALVED

1½ CUP WALNUT HALVES

2 TABLESPOONS BROWN SUGAR

½ TEASPOON GROUND CINNAMON

2 TABLESPOONS TAWNY PORT

1 TABLESPOON WILDFLOWER HONEY (OR CLOVE HONEY)

1 TABLESPOON FRESH MINT, CHOPPED

6 TABLESPOONS GREEK YOGURT

Preheat grill on medium heat.

In a large sauté pan over medium heat, melt the butter. Just as the butter begins to melt, add the apples and toss to coat. Remove the apples with a slotted spoon and set aside. Add the walnuts to the pan and toast until lightly browned, about 4 minutes. Add the brown sugar and the cinnamon, and mix vigorously, coating the nuts. Add the Port and let the mixture reduce for 4 minutes, stirring constantly. Add the honey and remove from heat.

Grill the apples for 5 minutes, or until the apple flesh shows dark grill marks. Let cool, and then dice. Add the apples back to the pan with the mint, and toss everything until it is well coated. Divide into six portions and serve in small bowls with a dollop of yogurt (about 1 tablespoon) over each.

BEVERAGE PAIRINGS

Beverage pairings need to be simple and forthright here. If you want to have a single pairing for the whole meal, then I strongly suggest a dry cider from Normandy. Its crisp and light apple flavors are phenomenal with all of the dishes in this chapter, especially the pork. Plus, its racy bubbles and low alcohol content make it perfect for eating outside on a hot day.

I am a fan of chilled sake at picnics, and a ginjo-shu sake with its clean and direct fruit flavors is fantastic alongside the watermelon salad. A favorite wine of mine is retsina, but be careful with that suggestion since most Americans hate it. It has a flavor of pine resin that can be overwhelming. What it will do—if you let it—is bring out a layer of ocean brine that accents the earthiness of the olives in the salad. For beer, go with a hefeweizen. The citrus and banana notes work really well with the juicy sweetness of the melon.

For the kebabs and the pork, the top choice is that bottle of French cider I mentioned earlier. For wine, a South African Chenin Blanc is my top choice: It has a waxy apple quality and a distinct minerality that brings out grill flavors extremely well. My favorite beer pairing goes in a totally different direction. An India pale ale from California, also known as IPA, brings a complex balance of sweet and bitter into the equation.

For the charoset, a slightly chilled LBV Port is my top choice. LBV is short for Late Bottle Vintage and denotes one of the best values in high-quality ruby Ports. The Port will mirror the rich flavors of the dessert. However, if it's too hot outside for Port, then go with a Moscato d'Asti, served well-chilled. If you want to go with a brew, then mead is the best choice; its honey notes accent the dessert beautifully.

AT THE BEACH, BY THE POOL

Is it unnerving how peaceful the beach can be? The crowds of tourists, the kids running around, all those boats out on the water—it should be a cacophony, yet you hear nothing but the waves, and within ten minutes of digging your feet into the sand your brain goes kaput.

The combination of sun and water can do strange things to the belly, too. A dinner at the beach or by the pool is more about snacking than a real meal. Food has to be light, but not so delicate that it can be ruined by some jostling or an errant bit of sand. And then there is the smell. The briny air off the ocean or the chlorine tang of the pool will dominate the senses. No matter how good your food smells, it's going to become partially lost in the aromas of the outdoors.

In the following recipes the smell of the air actually becomes part of the recipe. That might sound a little too much like molecular gastronomy, but it's really just common sense. Food tastes better in certain places; at the pool and at the beach, sharp and dramatic flavors work best. Another element that works really well is the charcoal grill. If you can, serve up the calamari to order off of a fiery grill. It's a perfect summer taste that no one will forget.

There are also some practical considerations for this meal. If you're at the beach, these dishes will probably be served out of plastic ware or some other portable container. For that reason, the following recipes are designed to look great even when scooped onto a paper plate without any fanfare.

Orange and Avocado Salad

It always amazes me how well opposites work together. The sweetness and spritzy acidity of the orange fits seamlessly with the creamy richness of the avocado. The feta cheese lends it much-needed saltiness. When cutting the avocado, try to mimic the size and shape of the orange segments. It will look really cool.

SERVES 4 TO 6

8 OUNCES MIXED SALAD GREENS

1 ORANGE, PEELED INTO SEGMENTS

1 AVOCADO, SLICED

2 TABLESPOONS EXTRA-VIRGIN OLIVE OIL

1 VIDALIA ONION (ABOUT ¼ CUP), SLIVERED

2 TABLESPOONS FETA CHEESE

Place the salad greens into a large mixing bowl. Add the orange segments, avocado slices, oil, and onion. Toss until the mixture is thoroughly blended. Sprinkle individual portions with the feta cheese just before serving.

Grilled Calamari with Jalapeños and Cilantro

This dish is perfectly spicy and delicious. It's tantalizing in a way that a day at the beach should be. Keep in mind, though, that everyone's idea of spicy is different—if it makes you sweat and your tongue feel a bit numb, then that's more than enough heat. Be sure to allow enough time for the calamari to marinate fully.

SERVES 4 TO 6

1 POUND CLEANED CALAMARI TUBES (ABOUT 1½ CUPS), PREFERABLY FRESH

6 JALAPEÑO PEPPERS WITH SEEDS, OR FEWER TO TASTE, ROUGHLY DICED

1 BUNCH CILANTRO (ABOUT ½ CUP), ROUGHLY CHOPPED WITH STEMS

½ CUP FRESHLY SQUEEZED LEMON JUICE (ABOUT 3 LARGE LEMONS)

2 TABLESPOONS EXTRA-VIRGIN OLIVE OIL

1 TEASPOON TOASTED SESAME OIL

1 TEASPOON SOY SAUCE

If using wooden skewers, soak in water for 30 minutes.

In a large bowl, toss the calamari, peppers, cilantro, lemon juice, olive oil, sesame oil, and soy sauce together. Place the mixture in a resealable plastic bag or container. Marinate for 6 hours.

Preheat a grill on medium heat.

With at least a dozen skewers on hand, skewer the calamari lengthwise and grill, about 2 minutes on each side. Serve immediately.

Edamame Lubia (a.k.a. Soy Hummus)

This recipe takes hummus and amplifies everything that is good about it. It becomes easier, tastier, and healthier when made with soy beans. Since the word "hummus" is the Arabic term for chickpeas, I call this a *lubia*, Arabic for "bean," instead. Make sure the edamame are precooked. Otherwise, follow the package directions for blanching the pods before attempting to shell them.

SERVES 4 TO 6

1 POUND FROZEN EDAMAME PODS (ABOUT 4 CUPS)
1 TABLESPOON LEMON JUICE
1 CLOVE GARLIC, MINCED
1 TABLESPOON KOSHER SALT
1 TEASPOON FRESHLY GROUND BLACK PEPPER
2 TABLESPOONS SESAME OIL
1 POUND PITA BREAD, EACH PIECE QUARTERED

For the edamame, follow the package directions for blanching. Allow to cool, then shell. Purée the shelled beans (approximately 1 cup) in a food processor with the lemon juice, garlic, salt, pepper, sesame oil, and ½ cup water until well-blended. The end result should have the consistency of fresh ricotta cheese. Scoop into a serving bowl, arrange the pita bread on a tray, and serve.

Coconut Milk Panna Cotta with Cilantro Syrup

A classic and simple Tuscan dessert with a Thai twist. The key to panna cotta lies in making sure the gelatin sets properly. If you don't like cilantro, you can replace it with basil or mint. The syrup may be made up to two weeks in advance and refrigerated in an airtight container until ready to use. You will need custard cups or five-ounce ramekins, although small paper cups will work in a pinch.

SERVES 6

Panna Cotta

4 CUPS HEAVY CREAM

1 CAN (13.5 OUNCES) COCONUT MILK

¼ TEASPOON FINE SALT

½ CUP GRANULATED SUGAR

½ TEASPOON GROUND CARDAMOM

2 TEASPOONS VANILLA EXTRACT

1 TABLESPOON VEGETABLE OIL

2 PACKETS (ABOUT 4½ TEASPOONS) POWDERED, UNFLAVORED GELATIN

6 TABLESPOONS COLD WATER

Cilantro Syrup

1 CUP GRANULATED SUGAR

½ CUP FRESH CILANTRO LEAVES, CHOPPED

For the panna cotta: Heat the heavy cream, coconut milk, salt, and sugar in a saucepan over medium heat, making sure that the mixture does not come to a boil. Once the sugar is dissolved, remove the pan from the heat. Stir in the cardamom and the vanilla extract. Set aside.

Lightly oil six custard cups with vegetable oil. Set aside.

In a large bowl, whisk together the gelatin and the cold water, and let stand for 5 minutes, or until the mixture thickens and the gelatin starts to dissolve. Pour the very warm, heavy cream mixture over the gelatin and stir until the gelatin is completely dissolved.

Divide the panna cotta mixture among the prepared cups, then chill them until firm, at least 3 hours.

To make the syrup: Combine the sugar and 1 cup of water in a 1-quart saucepan. Place the pan over medium heat and stir to help the sugar dissolve. Let the mixture simmer until it has started to thicken, about 2 minutes. Remove from the heat and add the chopped cilantro. Allow the syrup to cool for 15 minutes, then strain it through a fine mesh sieve, and discard the cilantro.

Spoon a ½ tablespoon of the syrup on the top of each panna cotta cup and serve.

BEVERAGE PAIRINGS

Let's not get too fancy for a waterside dinner. A case of cheap lager is perfect. The trick to making it special is to sprinkle a little salt, or even orange zest, on the rim of the glasses. Salt works magic on cheap beer: it cuts the bitterness and draws a creamy sweetness to the front of the palate. Also, make sure to serve the beer ice-cold or else it will taste bitter. Even if you opt for my more elaborate pairings, you should still pair a cheap lager with the salad as it does an exceptional job of amping up the orange notes of the dish.

For the calamari, selecting a white wine with very high acidity but low alcohol is the key to a perfect pairing. A low alcohol content is important so that it doesn't clash with the fiery quality of the jalapeños. High acidity brings a crispness that refreshes the palate. Txakoli from the Basque region of Spain is the classic choice.

For the "hummus" we want a bright fresh white wine, too, but for very different reasons. Instead of moderating heat, this time we are using it to lighten up the dish. You can stick with the Txakoli, or switch over to a Pinot Grigio from the Alto Adige region of Italy.

With the panna cotta, a Canadian ice wine is a great match. It accents the freshness of the panna cotta and adds an exotic element to the sauce. However, my best pairing recommendation is a Belgian tripel ale, which adds spicy fruit flavors to the experience.

Cilantro-Mint Mojito

For a fun change I have an East-meets-West inspired cocktail. Well, perhaps it's more of a West Indies-meets-South Asia cocktail, but I digress. This mojito works really well with a waterside dinner or as a stand-alone drink while sunbathing.

SERVES 1

2 TEASPOONS SODA WATER, DIVIDED
3 FRESH MINT SPRIGS, DIVIDED
2 CILANTRO LEAVES
2 TEASPOONS GRANULATED SUGAR
1 OUNCE FRESHLY SQUEEZED LIME JUICE (ABOUT 1 LIME)
2 OUNCES WHITE RUM
CRACKED ICE CUBES

In a mixing glass, add a dash of soda water (about 1 teaspoon) with 2 mint sprigs, the cilantro, and the sugar. Muddle the mixture until the sugar dissolves completely and you can smell the mint.

Squeeze the lime juice into the glass, add the rum, and shake with ice.

Strain over cracked ice into a highball glass.

Top with the remaining soda water, garnish with a mint sprig, and serve.

DINNER UNDER THE STARS

The end of summer is close at hand. The nights are cooling down, but daylight still shines late into the evening. The chance to dine *al fresco* is a transitory pleasure, so take it.

This meal is the final hurrah before autumn, the final dinner party before we go back to eating starchy root vegetables and wearing bulky sweaters. We are going to dine on perfect examples of flora and fauna tonight: this is the harvest feast.

Most of the courses here are served raw or slightly marinated. This style of preparation lets the extraordinary flavors of pitch-perfect summer ingredients shine. This meal cannot be made at any other time of the year, and the key is selecting the very best ingredients.

The best doesn't mean photo-ready, however. Farm fresh vegetables will be misshapen, crusty with dirt, with leaves eaten by bugs. These are living things plucked from the earth or a tree limb, ideally that very morning. You should be able to see their ties to nature in your hands. These visual markers will cue you to find that moment of perfect ripeness.

Fruits and vegetables are not the only seasonal produce; in fact, so is salmon. This is the time of year that wild salmon return to spawn in rivers from the Northern Pacific to Alaska. For our dish, I suggest seeking out Coho salmon. It has the perfect balance of lightness and color for the ceviche. Better yet, its habitats are well-managed and sustainably fished.

Finally, let's talk about the chef's role for this dinner. Most of the prep work can be done ahead of time, so you can spend the entire evening celebrating the end of the season with friends. The only dish that needs to be made to order is dessert. This is such a crowd-pleaser, though, that you're sure to be joined in the kitchen with guests willing to lend a hand.

Tomato and Peach Salad

These two fruits are at their peak of ripeness by the end of August. While it may sound crazy, tomatoes and peaches work together really well, and especially when both are extra-ripe. Mixing in an heirloom yellow tomato makes for a compelling composition on the plate. This can be prepared up to three hours ahead of time.

SERVES 4 TO 6

2 LARGE TOMATOES, CUT INTO WEDGES
2 LARGE PEACHES, PITTED AND CUT INTO WEDGES
1 SMALL VIDALIA ONION, CUT INTO WEDGES
    (ABOUT ¼ CUP)
2 TABLESPOONS FRESHLY SQUEEZED LIME JUICE
    (ABOUT 1 LIME)
1 JALAPEÑO PEPPER, DICED
¼ CUP EXTRA-VIRGIN OLIVE OIL
1 BUNCH CILANTRO (ABOUT ½ CUP), FINELY CHOPPED
1 TABLESPOON KOSHER SALT
1 TEASPOON FRESHLY GROUND BLACK PEPPER

In a large mixing bowl, combine the tomatoes, peaches, and onion. Toss together, then add the lime juice, jalapeño, olive oil, cilantro, salt, and pepper. Mix until the tomatoes and peaches become thoroughly coated.

Salmon Ceviche with Crispy Chickpeas

Classic ceviche is a traditional curing method using salt, spice, and lemon juice. Modern ceviche is a very different type of dish; instead of curing, the citrus and chiles are used to highlight the bright flavor of the fish. This can be prepped up in advance, but keep the fish and the sauce separated until a few minutes before serving.

SERVES 4 TO 6

⅓ CUP FRESHLY SQUEEZED LIME JUICE
    (ABOUT 2 LIMES)
1 JALAPEÑO, SEEDED AND DICED
1 SPANISH ONION (ABOUT 1 CUP), DICED
1 AVOCADO, HALVED, PITTED, PEELED, AND FINELY
    CHOPPED
1 BUNCH CILANTRO (ABOUT ½ CUP), FINELY CHOPPED
1 TEASPOON SOY SAUCE
8 OUNCES COHO SALMON FILLET, FINELY DICED

In a large bowl, mix the lime juice, jalapeño, onion, avocado, cilantro, and soy sauce. Carefully toss with the salmon until the fish is thoroughly coated. Let sit for 3 minutes, allowing the salmon to absorb the marinade. Serve immediately with Crispy Chickpeas (recipe follows).

Crispy Chickpeas

The traditional accompaniment to ceviche might surprise you: popcorn, which acts as a natural counterpoint to cured fish, lends a satisfying contrast in texture. In our menu, the crispy chickpeas offer the same dynamic while introducing an exotic flavor to the addictive crunch.

SERVES 4 TO 6
   (ALONGSIDE SALMON CEVICHE)
1 (16-OUNCE) CAN CHICKPEAS
2 TABLESPOONS EXTRA-VIRGIN OLIVE OIL
1 TEASPOON SEA SALT
2 TEASPOONS CURRY POWDER

Drain, rinse, and dry the chickpeas. Preheat oven to 400°F. In a mixing bowl, combine the chickpeas, olive oil, salt, and curry until thoroughly combined. Spread the mixture onto a sheet pan and roast the chickpeas for about 40 minutes, shaking the pan every 10 minutes, until they turn crispy. They are best served immediately but can be stored in an airtight container for up to one week.

Beef Carpaccio

This is a modern classic that has been embraced by chefs throughout Europe. Ask your butcher for a center cut of beef tenderloin for this dish. To serve the meat paper-thin, place it in the freezer for two hours, or until it starts to harden. You will still need a very sharp chef's knife to cut through the tenderloin but it'll be much easier to slice after freezing.

SERVES 4 TO 6
8 OUNCES BEEF FILLET, CUT VERY THINLY
2 TABLESPOONS FRESHLY SQUEEZED LEMON JUICE
   (ABOUT 1 LARGE LEMON)
1 TABLESPOON KOSHER SALT
1 TEASPOON FRESHLY GROUND BLACK PEPPER
2 TEASPOONS EXTRA-VIRGIN OLIVE OIL
3 OUNCES (ABOUT ½ CUP) FRESH PARMESAN, THINLY
   SLICED
5 SPRIGS FRESH BASIL, STEMS REMOVED (OPTIONAL)

Arrange the thinly sliced beef on a large plate. Sprinkle the beef with about 1 tablespoon of the lemon juice, then flip the slices and sprinkle the other sides with the remaining lemon juice. Season with the salt and pepper. Refrigerate, covered, until ready to serve.

When ready to serve, drizzle the olive oil over the top, scatter the Parmesan and the basil leaves, and serve immediately.

Crempog with Poached Pear Sauce

Crempog is a traditional Welsh dessert perfect for late summer. This is essentially a small fluffy pan-fried cake, similar in texture to a shortcake. This dish is intended to cap off a late summer dinner when the nights are a bit cooler; its hearty sweetness also makes for a great breakfast.

SERVES 4 TO 6

Crempog
½ CUP SELF-RISING FLOUR
1½ TEASPOONS GRANULATED SUGAR
1 EGG
¼ CUP MILK, PLUS MORE AS NEEDED
1½ TEASPOONS UNSALTED BUTTER, MELTED

Poached Pear Sauce
1 CUP GRANULATED SUGAR
¼ CUP DRY WHITE WINE
4 MEDIUM PEARS (ABOUT 4 CUPS), PEELED AND SLIVERED
1 TEASPOON VANILLA EXTRACT
NONSTICK COOKING SPRAY

For the crempog: Sift the flour into a medium-sized bowl, and stir in the sugar. Make a well in the center of the dough, and add the egg. Stir the egg into the flour with a kitchen spoon while gradually pouring in the milk and the butter. The dough should be smooth; if not, add up to another ¼ cup of milk. Let sit for 30 minutes.

For the pear sauce: In a medium sauté pan, bring ¼ cup water, sugar, and wine to a boil for 5 minutes. Reduce heat; carefully add the pears and the vanilla. Cover and simmer for 3 minutes, or until tender.

Heat a skillet over medium heat. Coat with cooking spray. Drop large spoonfuls of the dough onto the hot skillet, placing them 2-inches apart in the pan. Flip each cake when bubbles appear on the surface of the dough, about 2 to 3 minutes, and cook until browned, about another 2 minutes, on the other side. Remove from pan and set aside.

Drizzle each hot cake with pear sauce, and serve immediately.

BEVERAGE PAIRINGS

Margarita

For the Tomato and Peach Salad, I want a South African Viognier from either the Paarl or Stellenbosch region. The wine mirrors the fresh peach flavors and adds a bit of honeysuckle and lemongrass to the mix. For beer, nothing goes better than a Mexican lager (which is actually a long-lost style from Vienna) due to its light and smooth qualities.

Take note that the iron in wine sometimes reacts with the fish oils to deliver a nasty after-taste. Pairing wine can be a little like a game of fish roulette. A good bet is a Pinot Noir from New Zealand; my very un-scientific studies lead me to believe they are the least likely to contain high iron levels. However, I turned up the spice element a bit in this dish, so a white wine will work perfectly, as will a margarita.

With the carpaccio I'm seeking an earthier wine, something with the vitality of ripe fruit but also the orange and almond notes of an older wine. Unless you have some old Burgundian Pinots kicking around, a Rioja Gran Reserva is the way to go. You can often purchase bottles that are a decade old at a reasonable price. An English brown ale is lovely, too, with its toast and bitter caramel notes bouncing off the seasoned beef.

The crempog adds a touch of warmth to the meal and so should the beverage pairing. Serve this dessert with a snifter of eau de vie de poire Williams, a brandy made from Bartlett pears. The flavors will match the flavors in the dessert, but also add notes of fresh roses and vanilla. When selecting a bottle remember that the best come from Alsace. Although you will find some with a pear bobbing in the bottle, ignore these—it's just an expensive gimmick.

The classic margarita is a great pairing with the ceviche. The sea salt on the rim will bring a smokiness to the fish. The tequila turns up the heat on those chiles, while the sweetness of the triple sec keeps it from getting out of control.

SERVES 1

ICE

1½ OUNCES AGAVE BLANCO TEQUILA

1 OUNCE FRESHLY SQUEEZED LIME JUICE
    (ABOUT 1 LIME)

½ OUNCE TRIPLE SEC

2 TABLESPOONS SEA SALT FOR RIMMING THE
    GLASS (OPTIONAL)

Fill a rocks glass with ice. Add the tequila, the lime juice, and the triple sec. Stir a few times until the mixture is completely chilled. If using salt, place the salt in a shallow dish, moisten the rim of another rocks glass with a dampened paper towel, then dip it in the dish. The rim should be thoroughly coated with salt. Strain cocktail into the new glass and serve.

AUTUMN

AUTUMN IS THE MOST NOSTALGIC OF SEASONS. Perhaps it's because we long for the endless days of summer. Perhaps it's because we are contemplating the long nights of winter that lay ahead. For cooks, it's often because our passionate flings with farm-fresh abundance are quickly drawing to a bitter end. After all, evening temperatures are dropping fast, and THE NEED FOR RICHER FARE IS REPLACING THE DESIRE FOR ZESTY, SUN-SOAKED SIMPLICITY.

Autumn is a great time of the year to cook although it can seem challenging to prepare dishes with seasonal fruits and vegetables. At first, the bounty of the summer is still at hand, satiating our need for color with ruby red apples, deep purple eggplants, knuckled carrots freshly pulled from the earth, and all variety of pepper saturated with rainbow intensity. Then, as the fall sinks in, the colors on the shelves become more muted. THE DUSTY BROWN OF POTATOES, THE TERRA COTTA HUE OF SQUASH, THE BLANCHED TONES OF CAULIFLOWER OR ONION—ALTHOUGH BEAUTIFUL IN THEIR OWN RIGHT—SIMPLY DON'T INSPIRE INNOVATION IN THE KITCHEN IN QUITE THE SAME WAY. In fact, this transition to a much narrower palate of ingredients can be jarring for even the most experienced chef.

MY RECIPES FOR THIS TIME OF YEAR ARE A PLAYFUL MIX OF NOSTALGIA AND INNOVATIVE FLAVORS USING INGREDIENTS AT THEIR PEAK DURING THE FALL MONTHS. You will find a celebration of fungi, root vegetables, and fall greens throughout this chapter. My goal is to replicate meals of my childhood in New England where I experienced most of these vegetables for the first time. Fortunately for you, I also remember how bland and flavorless the food was—I was a teenager the first time I tasted garlic. THE RESULTING RECIPES ARE A FUSION IN THE BEST POSSIBLE WAY, of both memory and palate, and will keep your guests happy and enchanted as the earth tilts towards yet another winter season.

AUTUMN DINNER PARTY

Everyone should have a reputation. Yours should be for hosting great parties. The trick is not to concern yourself with achieving perfection. Dinner parties are not meant to revolve around profound or complex food that rivals a three-star restaurant. (If you think your friends demand perfection, then you either need new friends or a few years in therapy.) The important thing is that the food is tasty, there is a sense of playfulness and, most importantly, that the dishes are largely prepared ahead of time. The main principle at work is to provide an environment of comfort and joviality for everyone, including yourself.

A while ago I was at a dinner party with a dear friend who happens to be a restaurant critic. Also at the table sat one of those bitter foodies who believe that making homemade quince paste is somehow a mark of superiority. The cook for this meal? The critic's poor wife, who had opted for a very French and elaborate six course meal—the kind that usually involves a team of chefs to prep the food and cook each dish with unerring skill. That no one got divorced, shot, or otherwise abused that night is a miracle. I've had meetings with my accountant that were less stressful than that dinner.

While it may seem that the only way to impress your friends is to host elaborate dinners, the reality is that if the food is satisfying and everyone is relaxed, it's going to be a great time. Simply put, food tastes better when you (or your guests) are not stressed out.

For this party, I have created a "China-via-Maine" theme. It's a bit crazy, really delicious, and a lot of fun. Your guests will be chomping on a rather authentic Szechuan classic, the hot pot, but instead of a pot full of hot broth (sure to cause mayhem, if not a hospital visit) we will be using an old-fashioned electric griddle, the kind a New Englander like me traditionally uses to cook pancakes. For some reason, I always think of New England when I think of an electric griddle, hence the name of this quirky dish.

New England Hot Pot

The hot pot is a classic dish from southern China, one that allows everyone to have exactly what they want to eat, flavored just the way they like it. The spicier the better! The classic Szechuan dish is hotter than you can imagine.

SERVES 6

2 CUPS VEGETABLE OIL

1 CUP SOY SAUCE, PREFERABLY NATURALLY AGED

1 CUP UNSEASONED RICE WINE VINEGAR

6 TO 8 GARLIC CLOVES (ABOUT ¼ CUP), MASHED

1 TABLESPOON CRUSHED RED PEPPER FLAKES

¼ CUP SZECHUAN PEPPERCORNS (OR BLACK PEPPER-
   CORNS)

1 POUND DRIED GLASS NOODLES (OR DRIED VERMI-
   CELLI NOODLES)

2 PARSNIPS, SLICED INTO 1-INCH-THICK STRIPS

2 TURNIPS, SLICED INTO 1-INCH-THICK STRIPS

2 PORTABELLA MUSHROOMS, SLICED INTO 1-INCH-
   THICK STRIPS, INCLUDING STEMS

10 MEDIUM-SIZED SHRIMP, PEELED AND DEVEINED

4 OUNCES BEEF TENDERLOIN, SLICED INTO THIN
   STRIPS

¼ CUP SPRING ONION (WHITE AND GREEN PARTS),
   DICED

¼ CUP UNSALTED ROASTED PEANUTS, CHOPPED

SZECHUAN CHILI PASTE (OR TABASCO SAUCE), FOR
   SEASONING

Arrange a spot for an electric griddle in the center of the table, allowing easy access for your guests. Preheat the griddle at its highest setting for about 15 minutes.

Make the sauce: In a large bowl, mix the vegetable oil, soy sauce, vinegar, mashed garlic, red pepper flakes, and the peppercorns until thoroughly blended. Set aside.

Prepare the noodles: Set a large pot of water on high heat, bring to a full boil, then add the noodles. Cook the noodles until tender, about 2 minutes. Drain and set aside.

Bring a second large pot of water to a boil, and cook the parsnips and turnips for about 4 minutes, strain, and plunge immediately into an ice bath for 3 minutes. Remove from the water and set aside.

Place the mushrooms, root vegetables, shrimp, and beef into separate serving dishes and drizzle the sauce over each ingredient, coating them thoroughly. Let marinate for 10 minutes, then arrange around the griddle.

Place the noodles, onions, peanuts, and chili paste in small bowls around the table as well: guests will garnish their prepared food with these ingredients. Also make the vegetable oil, soy sauce, garlic, and red pepper flakes available to everyone. Each person will blend his or her own dipping sauce with these ingredients in small, individual bowls arranged in front of each place setting.

Once everyone has made a dipping sauce, invite them to place their choice of meats and vegetables on the hot griddle. Cook the ingredients until each portion reaches the desired level of doneness, keeping in mind that each ingredient will only take a few minutes to fully cook. Guests will then dip the cooked food into their dipping sauce, allowing it to cool slightly before eating. Garnish with the noodles, onions, and peanuts, as desired.

AUTUMN DINNER PARTY

Snow Peas with Salt

Simply cooked snow peas are a fast and delicious accompaniment to any Asian-inflected meal. This is perfect either as a side dish for the hot pot, or as an appetizer to serve your guests while you prepare the main course.

SERVES 6

2 TABLESPOONS UNSALTED BUTTER
2 TEASPOONS KOSHER SALT
4 CUPS SNOW PEAS, STRINGS REMOVED

In a large sauté pan over medium heat, melt the butter. Add the salt and the snow peas. Reduce the heat to low, cover, and continue cooking for 1 minute, or just until the peas turn bright green. Serve immediately.

Maple Glazed Duck with Szechuan Peppercorns

Roasting a whole duck requires multiple steps, but the process is quite easy and the result—burnished skin and succulent, rich meat—is one of the best things you will ever eat. The secret to achieving perfectly crisp skin is to render a lot of the bird's natural fat. But don't discard it; we'll reserve the flavorful drippings for use in the Turducken (page 80).

SERVES 6

ONE 3 TO 5 POUND DUCK (PREFERABLY FRESH, BUT FROZEN AND THAWED IS FINE)
1 TABLESPOON FINE SALT
2 CUPS MAPLE SYRUP
1½ TEASPOONS CAYENNE PEPPER
1½ TEASPOONS GROUND CORIANDER
1 TABLESPOON SZECHUAN PEPPERCORNS (OR BLACK PEPPERCORNS), CRACKED
2 TABLESPOONS SOY SAUCE, PREFERABLY NATURALLY AGED

The night before you plan to serve the duck, wash the bird inside and out, removing the giblet bag if included in the cavity, and pat dry. (If you like, sauté the liver from the giblet bag in butter for a little chef snack.) Trim the duck of excess fat, and pierce the skin—but never the meat—dozens of times with a metal skewer or the tip of a paring knife. Rub the duck entirely with the salt, and let sit in a baking pan with a wire rack, breast-side up, in the refrigerator overnight.

Preheat oven to 325°F. Place the duck and pan into oven.

After 45 minutes, pull the duck out of the oven. Place the duck on a cutting board and poke the skin a dozen times—again making sure not to cut into the meat. Drain the rendered fat from the pan into a heatproof container. Turn over the duck and carefully place it back into the pan and return to the oven. Repeat five times, for a total roasting time of about 4 hours. (When all of the fat has been drained, seal the container, and store in the refrigerator for future use.)

Before the duck comes out of the oven, prepare the sauce. In a sauté pan over medium heat, add the maple syrup, cayenne pepper, coriander, peppercorns, and soy sauce, and stir for 3 minutes. Remove from heat.

Remove the duck from the oven, and increase the heat to 425°F. Place the duck into a large metal mixing bowl. Slowly drizzle the sauce over the duck, coating the duck entirely.

Return the duck to the roasting pan, breast side up, and cook for another 20 minutes, or until the glaze is a dark, golden-brown and the skin becomes crispy. Transfer the duck to a carving board and let rest for 15 minutes before serving.

Lemongrass and Ginger Granita

Granita is the lovechild of sorbet and Italian ice. Its texture is a little less refined than sorbet, but doesn't require as much hassle to make at home. This dessert continues the motif of East-meets-West and delicately balances the sweet and savory notes in the previous dishes.

SERVES 6

2 STALKS LEMONGRASS

1 TEASPOON FINE SALT

1 TEASPOON RED PEPPER FLAKES

2 TABLESPOONS GINGER, CHOPPED

2 CUPS GRANULATED SUGAR

½ CUP FRESHLY SQUEEZED LEMON JUICE (ABOUT 3 LARGE LEMONS)

½ CUP FRESHLY SQUEEZED LIME JUICE (ABOUT 4 LIMES)

In a medium sauté pan over high heat, combine the lemongrass, salt, red pepper flakes, ginger, sugar, and 3½ cups of water. Bring to a boil, then remove the mixture from the heat and let cool to room temperature.

When the mixture is cool, add the lemon juice and the lime juice. Strain the liquid, discarding solids, and place the mixture into a large bowl and place in the freezer.

Stir every 30 minutes until the mixture becomes evenly frozen, about 2 hours, making sure to scrape the ice crystals from the sides of the bowl as you stir. Scoop into individual serving bowls and serve immediately.

BEVERAGE PAIRINGS

With the hot pot, you better be drinking lager and plenty of it. This dish is so spicy that you really can't have wine or cocktails. It's actually a good idea to serve a nonalcoholic drink as well, like chilled black tea or coconut water. With the duck, a Syrah from the Santa Lucia Highlands in California would be top notch, but those are hard to find; one from Santa Barbara would be great, too.

Black Pepper Martini

When preparing an exotic dinner I like to greet guests at the door with something slightly off-beat, like this black pepper martini, to liven up their palates.

SERVES 1

ICE CUBES

3 OUNCES GIN

½ OUNCE DRY VERMOUTH

3 WHOLE SZECHUAN PEPPERCORNS (OR BLACK PEPPERCORNS), FOR GARNISH

Fill cocktail shaker with ice, add the gin and vermouth. Shake and strain into a chilled martini glass. Drop in the peppercorns and serve.

SUNDAY SUPPER

The joyous cacophony of the Sunday supper is a great American tradition: The ripple of old jokes, the chirping of new stories, the cling-clang-cling of glasses. I find that people are happiest sitting at a table with good friends, spooning out ample portions of simple dishes, and pouring big glasses of uncomplicated beverages.

I descend from decades of teetotaling New England ministers, so I was into my teens before witnessing the magic of this traditional family gathering. At the time I was working at a fine dining restaurant in Boston. One Sunday, just after finishing service, my chef insisted that I and a few other of the kitchen rats join him at his home for an Italian dinner.

Before that night, Sunday supper was a quiet and grim affair of gray vegetables and a meatloaf of questionable origin. That evening, though, I was treated to a risotto with fresh porcini mushrooms, each creamy grain of rice exploding with spell-binding savoriness. As I sat there—reveling in my first gastronomic trance—bottles of wine and laughter were passed across the table in equal measure. Since that day, I've held fast to the belief that the most nourishing meal is shared with family, whether you are related or not.

One of the best cuisines for bringing people together hails from the Italian region of Tuscany. This type of fare is wholesome and satisfying, as well as simple to prepare. It's hard to sit down to this meal and not laugh and talk until late in the evening.

The hallmarks of this dinner include hearty beans, seasonal mushrooms, and salad greens, along with rustic preparations for both the main entrée and dessert. You will soon notice, however, that there's no mention of tomato sauce in this chapter. There is a good reason for that: tomato sauce is common in Southern Italy, not in Tuscany. Also, at this time of year those tomatoes sitting on grocery store shelves aren't very appetizing—one more reason Tuscan cuisine is my top choice for an autumnal meal.

Warm Salad of Spinach and Pan-Roasted Mushrooms

Salad is too often treated like jury duty—a begrudged necessity. Let's prove that stereotype wrong. The crispy bacon and toothsome mushrooms here are decadent little treats hidden within warm spinach leaves scented with garlic. The most important ingredient is the anchovy: It adds a mysteriously delicious flavor that will have everyone going for seconds.

SERVES 6

1 TABLESPOON EXTRA-VIRGIN OLIVE OIL

2 ANCHOVY FILLETS, MINCED

4 TO 6 SLICES BACON (ABOUT 1 CUP), CUT INTO THIN STRIPS

2 TABLESPOONS GARLIC, CRUSHED

1 LARGE SPANISH ONION (ABOUT 1½ CUPS), DICED

1 POUND SHIITAKE OR PORTABELLA MUSHROOM CAPS (ABOUT 4 CUPS), HALVED, CUT INTO ¼-INCH-THICK SLICES

1 TABLESPOON BALSAMIC VINEGAR

1 POUND BABY SPINACH (ABOUT 6 CUPS)

1 TEASPOON FRESHLY GROUND BLACK PEPPER

In a hot sauté pan over medium-high heat, add the olive oil, anchovies, and bacon. Cook, stirring occasionally, for about 5 minutes, or until the bacon has rendered much of its fat, becoming extra-crispy. Add the garlic and the onion to the pan, and stir. Cook for another 2 minutes or until the onion softens and begins to turn translucent, about 3 minutes. Stir the mixture vigorously, then push the ingredients to the edges of the pan.

Add the mushrooms to the center of the pan. Cook undisturbed for 3 minutes, or until the mushrooms start to caramelize. Turn the mushrooms over, and toss the mixture together. Add the balsamic vinegar, then remove from the heat. In a large bowl, combine the spinach and the mushroom mixture. Add the black pepper and stir to combine. Serve immediately.

Fresh Orecchiette with Green Pea Cream

This pasta dish balances the fresh flavors of peas and parsley with the porky goodness of a bacon-cream sauce. While the sauce is easy to make, the pasta can seem a bit challenging for the novice cook. I have created a very simple pasta recipe here with beginners in mind. While it does require some practice, the results are worth it. If you want to skip making the pasta, substitute a pound of dry penne or farfalle instead.

SERVES 4 AS AN ENTRÉE
OR 6 AS AN APPETIZER

Fresh Orecchiette (Pasta)
2 CUPS SEMOLINA FLOUR
3 CUPS UNBLEACHED ALL-PURPOSE FLOUR, DIVIDED
1 CUP LUKEWARM WATER, DIVIDED

Green Pea Cream Sauce
2 SLICES BACON, CUT INTO SHORT, THIN STRIPS
1 SHALLOT, DICED
2 CUPS HEAVY CREAM
½ CUP FROZEN GREEN PEAS
1 TEASPOON WHITE PEPPER
1 TABLESPOON ITALIAN PARSLEY, FINELY CHOPPED
2 TABLESPOONS GRATED PARMESAN
CHOPPED ITALIAN PARSLEY, FOR GARNISH

For the fresh pasta: Add the semolina flour, 2 cups all-purpose flour, and ½ cup of the water to the work bowl of a food processor. Pulse the mixture for 2 minutes. Let rest for 1 minute. Add the remainder of the water and pulse for another 2 minutes, until the dough is firm.

Using a spatula, push the dough onto a cutting board dusted with flour (use the remaining 1 cup of all-purpose flour for dusting). Form the dough into a ball and wrap in plastic wrap. Let rest for 30 minutes.

Unwrap the dough onto a flour-dusted cutting board and cut into 3 pieces. Roll out each piece into a log about as wide as a wine cork. You can wrap up the pasta again at this point and store it in the refrigerator for three to four days.

For the sauce: In a small sauce pan over medium-high heat, cook the bacon until the fat has rendered and it has begun to brown, about 2 to 4 minutes, and then add the shallot. Sauté until the shallot has caramelized, about 2 minutes. Pull the pan off the heat and add the cream. Put the pan back on the heat and bring to a boil. Boil for 3 minutes, stirring slowly to make sure the mixture does not boil over as the sauce thickens. Add the peas and white pepper, and return to a boil, letting the sauce reduce for another 2 minutes, or until it starts to thicken slightly. Add the parsley and grated cheese, and remove from heat; cover to keep warm.

For the pasta: Fill a large pot halfway with salted water, place over high heat, and bring to a boil.

Slice the logs of pasta into ¼-inch rounds. (Dusting your knife with flour will help it from sticking to the dough.) Press your thumb gently into the center of each pasta round. The result should look like a little ear, which is the meaning of *orecchiette* in Italian. Drop the pasta into the boiling water, a small handful at a time. As soon as the pasta rises to the top (about 1 minute), scoop out with a slotted spoon into a large serving bowl and cover to keep warm.

Toss the pasta and sauce together. The sauce should barely coat the pasta. For the best presentation, sprinkle a touch of parsley over the bowl just before serving.

Pork Chops with Sage and White Beans

One of the hallmarks of Italian cooking is balance. In this dish, adding a touch of lemon adds vivacity to the earthy flavors of pork, fried sage, and garlic.

SERVES 6

6 BONELESS PORK CHOPS (ABOUT 6 OUNCES EACH)

2 TABLESPOONS EXTRA-VIRGIN OLIVE OIL, DIVIDED

1 TABLESPOON FINE SALT

1 TABLESPOON FRESHLY GROUND BLACK PEPPER

4 GARLIC CLOVES, SLICED

6 FRESH SAGE LEAVES

2 TABLESPOONS LEMON JUICE

2 CUPS CANNED WHITE BEANS (CANNELLINI OR GREAT NORTHERN), DRAINED AND RINSED

1 TABLESPOON CHOPPED ITALIAN PARSLEY, PLUS SPRIGS FOR GARNISH

Coat each pork chop with ¼ tablespoon of the olive oil and ½ teaspoon each of salt and pepper, and set aside. Place a large sauté pan over medium-high heat, add the remaining olive oil, garlic, and sage to the pan and cook for 1 minute, until the garlic starts to brown and the sage crisps. Carefully remove the sage and garlic from the oil, and reserve.

Add the pork chops to the hot pan and cook undisturbed for 4 minutes, or until the meat turns deep golden-brown. Flip the chops, and cook about 2 minutes more, or until an instant-read thermometer reads 145°F. Remove the pork chops from the pan, and reduce the heat to low.

Return the fried garlic and sage to the pan, and add the lemon juice. Scrape the bottom of the pan with a wooden spoon to release any crispy bits (the tasty stuff!) and then add the beans. Toss together, and cook until the beans are warmed through.

Place one pork chop and a single scoop of beans on each plate. Garnish with parsley, and serve at once.

Tuscan Cheesecake

This cheesecake uses ricotta cheese instead of cream cheese, which offers a softer texture and more nuanced flavors. I like to serve individual portions in the ramekins in which they were baked for a rustic presentation.

SERVES 6

2 TABLESPOONS BLANCHED SLIVERED ALMONDS

1 TEASPOON GRATED LEMON ZEST

1½ CUPS RICOTTA CHEESE

4 LARGE EGG YOLKS

½ CUP GRANULATED SUGAR

1 TABLESPOON UNSALTED BUTTER, FOR GREASING RAMEKINS

1 TABLESPOON SHAVED CHOCOLATE, FOR GARNISH

Preheat oven to 350°F. In a food processor, pulse the almonds and lemon zest until the almonds become finely ground. Add the ricotta, egg yolks, and sugar, and pulse until creamy.

Grease six 4-ounce ramekins with butter. Divide the mixture evenly among the ramekins, filling each two-thirds full. Bake for 30 minutes, or until light golden-brown. Garnish each cake with the chocolate shavings just before serving. Serve warm in ramekins, one per guest.

BEVERAGE PAIRINGS

The briny flavors of the salad pair perfectly with the fragrant citrus of a Fiano di Avellino, a pretty white wine from Southern Italy. A great beer pairing is an Irish stout; its malty tones accent the caramelized mushrooms seamlessly.

Two good pairings for the pasta course include a Pinot Noir from New Zealand and a brown ale from England. The Pinot gives the bacon-laced sauce an added dimension of freshness and really cements the marriage of the peas and bacon. The ale, on the other hand, brings a touch of toasty sweetness to the mix, making the cream sauce even more decadent.

For the pork chops, a red Tuscan wine is the smartest pairing. The most famous such wine would be Chianti, and that is a safe bet for this dish. However, I suggest looking for a Morellino di Scansano. It has a bit more heft than Chianti and is often a better value. If you can't find a Morellino, see if you can locate a Rosso Piceno, which is another lovely food-friendly red from central Italy. For the resolute beer drinker in the group, a hearty India pale ale is the top choice.

Dessert is essential at a Sunday supper, but a sweet wine is not. Your best dessert wine with this dense cake is a sweet and savory Vin Santo del Chianti Classico. However, a sparkling wine like Prosecco would be even more fun: the bubbles will freshen up the palate after each sip. For a great beer pairing, try a framboise lambic from Belgium.

THANKSGIVING

Thanksgiving folds family, friends, and culture into the biggest, baddest, most beauteous dinner of the year. The triumvirate of turkey, cranberries, and stuffing has held its ground since the beginning of our shared history as Americans. It has remained shockingly unscathed against the tides of religion, politics, jingoism, and marketing for the past four hundred years.

This holiday, then, is a microcosm of America at her best. Every family and every culture has reinterpreted the celebration, yet it somehow remains intact. On the fourth Thursday of November—no matter the particular style of the cuisine served—we all sit down to an honest-to-goodness Thanksgiving dinner.

The melting pot of our country has created some wildly exotic and wonderful Thanksgiving meals, and I crave each and every one of them! From a Jamaican family I discovered how easily the tartness of cranberries can sink into that Caribbean specialty—rum. In the South I learned the frighteningly addictive quality of deep fried turkey with chitterlings. I also know for a fact that every one of my gay friends can turn Thanksgiving into a fabulous brunch. Cranberry cosmo, anyone?

In this chapter, I have created a menu that keeps those classic flavors in place while mixing in innovative elements, too. The stuffing with lavender is a personal favorite.

Oyster Stew

A very straightforward—and incredibly delicious—dish that relies on speed. This has to be cooked and served immediately for the flavors and textures to remain intact. You don't have to shuck your own oysters for this dish; many grocery stores sell them pre-shucked.

SERVES 6

2 SHALLOTS, FINELY DICED

1 TABLESPOON UNSALTED BUTTER

¼ CUP WHITE WINE

2 CUPS HEAVY CREAM

1 DOZEN SHUCKED OYSTERS

1 TABLESPOON ITALIAN PARSLEY, DICED

1 PINCH FINE SALT

Using a sauté pan, sauté the shallots with the butter over medium-high heat until translucent, about 2 minutes. Add the white wine, and reduce until it mostly evaporates, about 3 minutes. Add the cream, bringing the mixture to a boil, then add the oysters. As soon as the cream returns to a light boil—no more than 90 seconds—add the parsley and the salt. Serve immediately.

Turducken

The traditional turducken is an odd creation: a chicken stuffed inside a duck which is then stuffed into a turkey. My version uses just the essence of duck and chicken to accent the flavors of turkey to surprisingly delicious results. Refer to the Maple Glazed Duck with Szechuan Peppercorns recipe (page 64) for instructions on making rendered duck fat.

SERVES 6

½ CUP RENDERED DUCK FAT, DIVIDED

2 TABLESPOONS EXTRA-VIRGIN OLIVE OIL

5 GARLIC CLOVES, MINCED

¼ CUP SPANISH ONION, FINELY CHOPPED

½ TEASPOON FINE SALT

1 TEASPOON FRESHLY GROUND BLACK PEPPER

½ TEASPOON FRESH ROSEMARY, CHOPPED

¼ CUP CELERY, FINELY CHOPPED

ZEST OF 1 LEMON

½ CUP FRESH BREADCRUMBS

2 CUPS CHICKEN STOCK

1 (2 TO 3 POUND) TURKEY BREAST

Preheat your oven to 400°F.

In a sauté pan over medium heat, combine 1 tablespoon of the duck fat and the olive oil. Once the fat has melted, add the garlic, onions, salt, and pepper and sauté until onions are translucent, about 2 minutes. Add the rosemary, celery, lemon zest, and breadcrumbs and toss until coated. Add the chicken stock and bring to a boil. Simmer until the mixture has thickened to the consistency of bread pudding. Let cool for 20 minutes.

With a very sharp chef's knife, and using a large cutting block, butterfly the turkey breast by holding down the breast and carefully slicing the meat in half horizontally, with your knife parallel to the cutting board. Do not cut the entire way through. The end result should look something like the front and back pages of a magazine (albeit a magazine made of meat).

Flatten the butterflied turkey breasts, and pound them to a ½-inch thickness using either a meat tenderizer or the bottom of a heavy pot. Spread the stuffing on the turkey breast, leaving a ½-inch border all around. Starting at a long end, roll the turkey and stuffing to form a uniform log, then tie in four places with kitchen twine to secure the meat while it cooks.

Coat the turkey with the remaining duck fat, place on a sheet tray, and bake for 1 hour and 20 minutes, until the internal temperature reaches 165°F. Let rest for 10 minutes. To serve, remove the string and cut into one-inch-thick portions.

Savory Cranberry Stuffing

Stuffing is a staple. This one takes traditional Thanksgiving ingredients—stuffing, cranberries, and pecans—and transforms them into an alluring side dish with a note of lavender. Note that the bread should be slightly stale, so start preparing this the night before your feast.

SERVES 6

4 TABLESPOONS (½ STICK) UNSALTED BUTTER

2 GARLIC CLOVES, MASHED

1 SMALL SPANISH ONION (ABOUT ½ CUP), DICED

2 CUPS FRESH CRANBERRIES

1 TEASPOON DRIED LAVENDER FLOWERS

1 TABLESPOON FINE SALT

2 CUPS WHITE WINE

1 CUP BROWN SUGAR, LIGHTLY PACKED

1 CUP CHOPPED PECANS

2 CUPS MILK

5 LARGE EGGS, BEATEN

3 CUPS CUBED WHITE BREAD, ALLOWED TO SIT OUT IN
    A BOWL OVERNIGHT

Preheat the oven to 350°F. Melt the butter in a large sauté pan over medium-high heat and add the garlic, onion, and cranberries. Sauté until the onions turn translucent and begin to soften, about 2 minutes. Add the lavender, salt, and white wine, then simmer for about 3 minutes, until reduced by half. Add the brown sugar and pecans, and remove from the heat. Let cool for 20 minutes. Add the milk and eggs, and stir to combine. Pour this mixture over the cubed bread and let stand for 20 minutes.

Transfer the stuffing into a buttered 9 x 5-inch baking pan and bake for 35 minutes, or until dark golden-brown. Let cool to room temperature, then serve.

Creamed Pearl Onions with Peas and Carrots

This classic side dish was always my favorite dish during the holidays. It works on its own, but is even better when served on a plate with savory bread pudding and Turducken (see page 000).

SERVES 6

2 CUPS CHICKEN STOCK

1 POUND PEARL ONIONS (FRESH OR FROZEN), PEELED

1 LARGE CARROT (ABOUT ¼ POUND), DICED

½ CUP WHITE WINE

2 CUPS HEAVY CREAM

¼ POUND FROZEN GREEN PEAS, THAWED

In a medium pot over high heat, combine the chicken stock and 2 cups of water, and bring to a rapid boil. Add the onions, cook for 5 minutes, then add the carrots, and cook an additional 7 minutes, or until the water has reduced down to a thickened consistency.

Add the white wine, and boil another 12 minutes until the sauce becomes very thick. Add the heavy cream, bring to a boil, and reduce to a simmer for another 5 to 8 minutes. Bring the sauce to a boil once again and add the peas. Remove from the heat and serve.

Sweet Potato and Ginger Pie

The compulsory side dish of sweet potatoes gets a makeover here. The ginger marries extremely well with the more traditional spices, nutmeg and cinnamon, and injects this dessert with an exotic splash of flavor.

SERVES 6

3 SWEET POTATOES (ABOUT 3 CUPS), PEELED, CHOPPED INTO LARGE PIECES, BOILED AND MASHED

1 2-INCH PIECE GINGER, PEELED AND GRATED

¼ CUP GRANULATED SUGAR

1 TEASPOON VANILLA EXTRACT

¼ CUP LIGHT BROWN SUGAR, LIGHTLY PACKED

¼ TEASPOON GROUND NUTMEG

1 TEASPOON GROUND CINNAMON

¼ CUP SWEETENED CONDENSED MILK

1 TABLESPOON UNSALTED BUTTER, MELTED

2 LARGE EGGS, AT ROOM TEMPERATURE, LIGHTLY BEATEN

1 PREPARED PIE SHELL

½ CUP PECAN HALVES

Preheat oven to 375°F. In a large mixing bowl, combine the cooled sweet potato, ginger, sugar, vanilla, brown sugar, nutmeg, cinnamon, condensed milk, butter, and eggs until well mixed.

Pour the mixture into the prepared pie shell. Smooth the surface with the back of a spoon or spatula and decorate with pecan halves. Bake for 20 minutes until crust is golden-brown. Cool for 30 minutes, slice, and serve.

BEVERAGE PAIRINGS

With the creamy oyster stew, I like to serve a Pinot Blanc. This varietal is a bit richer than a Pinot Grigio and is armed with a bracing minerality that cuts through the richness of the oysters like a knife. I especially like the Pinot Blancs from Alsace. A great beer choice for the stew would be a Czech Pilsner, owing to its crisp and clean flavors.

The turducken balances bravado and finesse, and so should the wine. A Pinot Noir would work well—especially one from the Willamette Valley—but I think something a bit more exotic and festive would be a better fit. I personally love to serve an American wine from wine regions other than California. There are some good Cabernet Franc grapes being grown on the East Coast currently, particularly in New York and Pennsylvania. In the South (if you can call Virginia the South) there is some interesting Petit Verdot that would also complement the flavor profiles of this dish. In the Southwest, check out Arizona's Zinfandels for a fun change of pace.

The cranberry stuffing should be served with the turducken, and it will pair easily with the wine selection you chose from the above suggestions. Usually that's not the case with something like cranberries, but the lavender and onions soften up the tartness of the fruit, allowing the wine to unfold easily on the palate. The creamed onions, however, really should be paired with the Pilsner or Pinot Blanc.

For dessert, a milk stout is an exceptional pairing with sweet potato pie. The malty flavors of the beer effortlessly highlight the spices in the dish. For wines, a Gewürztraminer is the best bet, with its ginger-and-honeysuckle aromas modulating the eccentricity of the spices used in our preparation.

SAVORY BRUNCH

I admire folks who can jump out of bed at 8 a.m. on the weekend and speed out for a jog or clean up the house. I wish I had that much vim and vigor, because then I could easily whip up a great brunch first thing in the morning. But I can't.

I hate waking up early on the weekends, and I have a good excuse. Running a wine school means I often work nights. It doesn't help that my job requires me to taste wine. It probably also doesn't help that I firmly believe in having a beer or two after work and a glass of wine when I get home. Let's just say that I am in no shape to be handling knives before noon.

My trick is to have almost everything done a day or two in advance. Brunch is not a time for nuance; it's a fun event with bold flavors to wake up the palate, hearty foods to warm you on a chilly morning, and just enough booze to get everyone chatting and laughing. Food should be simple but offer an exciting combination of flavors.

For brunch, I am using more unusual ingredients than you'll typically find throughout this cookbook. Absinthe? How saucy! Black truffles? How daring! Bacon candy? How deliciously trashy! It's a trick I learned as a chef: using exotic ingredients is a great way to mask simple preparations.

With all the culinary fireworks going off, it will actually be the simplest dish—the scrambled eggs—that will steal the show. Perhaps the greatest lesson I learned from my years as a professional chef is this: there is nothing more satisfying than a perfectly scrambled egg.

Absinthe-Cured Salmon Gravlax

Curing with salt and sugar is a centuries-old method of preserving salmon. It also happens to be delicious. In this version, the dill and absinthe inject bold aromas of fresh flowers and herbs into the fish.

SERVES 6

2 SALMON FILLETS, ABOUT 1 POUND EACH
1½ TABLESPOONS FINE SALT
1 TABLESPOON GRANULATED SUGAR
1 TEASPOON FRESHLY GROUND BLACK PEPPER
1 BUNCH DILL (ABOUT ½ CUP), ROUGHLY CHOPPED
    WITH STEMS
1 TABLESPOON ABSINTHE (OR GIN)

Sprinkle the salmon fillets with the salt, sugar, and pepper, and then coat with dill and splash on the absinthe. Sandwich the fillets together and secure tightly in plastic wrap. Place the fish in a large zipped plastic bag, remove all air, and refrigerate. For best results, place a heavy item, such as a brick or tile, on top of the salmon while it rests on a plate in the refrigerator.

Once or twice a day for three days, pull the salmon out of the refrigerator and aggressively slosh around the juices in the bag. By the third full day of marinating, the fish will have fully cured. Remove from the bag, scrape off the seasoning and marinade, and discard. Slice the fish thinly on a bias. Serve with cream cheese and bagels.

The Perfect Scrambled Egg

The scrambled egg is a classic delight and should always be a simple affair. If you can find them, use eggs from a local farm; the yolks tend to be very orange and incredibly flavorful.

SERVES 6

6 LARGE EGGS
½ TEASPOON FINE SALT
2 TABLESPOONS UNSALTED BUTTER
CAVIAR, FOR SERVING
SHAVED BLACK TRUFFLES, FOR SERVING

Place a large, nonstick sauté pan over medium heat. In a large bowl, whisk the eggs and the salt with 2 tablespoons of water for 2 minutes, or until pale yellow. Add the butter to the pan. It should sizzle, but not smoke. As soon as the butter melts completely, add the egg mixture. Don't begin scrambling the egg right away. In about 1 minute, the eggs will start to stiffen, and that's your cue: With a heat-resistant spatula, move the slowly cooking eggs to the center of the pan, redistributing the runny egg to the outer edges.

Continue this motion as the eggs continue to set, breaking apart large curds as they form with your spatula. When the eggs are no longer runny, stir them once more and turn off the flame. Let them sit for 30 seconds, top with caviar and black truffles, then serve immediately.

Truffled Breakfast Empanadas with Artichokes

Hearty and filling, this empanada is the star of this brunch. It looks amazing, and your guests will delight in the aromas as they take their first forkful. The intense earthy scent of the truffle is awe-inspiring with the artichoke, now in season.

SERVES 6

2 TABLESPOONS UNSALTED BUTTER, PLUS MORE FOR GREASING THE BAKING SHEET

1 SPANISH ONION, DICED (ABOUT 1 CUP)

1 CUP (ABOUT 3 OUNCES) FRESH BUTTON MUSHROOMS, CHOPPED

1½ CUPS HEAVY CREAM

2 CUPS (ABOUT 14 OUNCES) ARTICHOKE HEARTS, QUARTERED

1 POUND FRESH BABY SPINACH (ABOUT 6 CUPS), ROUGHLY TORN INTO PIECES

1 TABLESPOON TRUFFLE OIL

½ TEASPOON FINE SALT

½ TEASPOON FRESHLY GROUND BLACK PEPPER

2 SHEETS OF DEFROSTED PUFF PASTRY (ABOUT 17 OUNCES)

3 LARGE EGG YOLKS BEATEN WITH ½ CUP COLD WATER

Melt the butter in a large pot over medium heat, and add the onions. Sauté the onions until they are translucent, about 2 to 3 minutes. Add the mushrooms and cook for about 3 minutes, then add the heavy cream and the artichoke hearts. (This filling can be made up to two days in advance and stored in the refrigerator.)

Once the mixture starts to boil, let it reduce for about 2 minutes. Toss in the spinach, turn off the heat, and give it a good stir. The consistency should be nice and thick. If it is still soupy, turn the heat back to medium and let it reduce some more. Once the texture is akin to that of cookie batter, add the truffle oil, salt, and pepper, and remove from the heat immediately. Let cool, and refrigerate overnight.

On the day of your brunch: Preheat the oven to 375°F. Flour a large cutting board, and lay out one sheet of the puff pastry. Roll it out to 12 x 18 inches. Cut the dough into six 6 x 6-inch squares and stack in a pile, making sure to flour between the squares to prevent them from sticking together. Repeat with the second puff pastry sheet. You should now have 12 squares of pastry.

Lay out one square. With a small knife, gently draw a line from one corner of the pastry to the opposite corner, making sure not to cut through the pastry. In the center of the bottom triangle, place ¼ cup of filling. Dip a finger in water and moisten the edges of the pastry. Fold the top triangle over the filling, pulling gently so the top and bottom edges meet. Use a fork to pinch and seal the edges.

Place the finished pockets on a buttered baking tray. Once you have completed all 12 empanadas, brush the tops with the egg-water mixture. Depending on the size of your oven, you may need to use two baking trays. Bake about 12 to 14 minutes, or until the empanadas are puffy and golden-brown.

Maple and Bourbon Bacon

Part dessert, part side dish, this brings together three of the greatest ingredients on earth. You will need a candy thermometer to make a soft maple candy coating for the bacon. Also, the syrup will need to be brought to an aggressive boil, so be careful when handling. The result will be toffee-coated slabs of boozy bacon. What could be better?

SERVES 6

12 SLICES BACON

2 TABLESPOONS BOURBON

½ CUP MAPLE SYRUP

In a large sauté pan over medium-low heat, render the bacon until it turns very crispy, about 15 minutes. Remove the bacon from the pan with a slotted spoon and set aside, on a plate covered with paper towels. Discard any remaining fat and deglaze the pan with the bourbon and 2 tablespoons of water. Swirl in the maple syrup, and return to the stove top, raising the heat to medium. Bring the syrup to a hard simmer, until it reaches 240°F, then return the bacon to the pan and coat with the syrup. Remove the pan from the heat, and lay out on a nonstick cookie sheet. Let cool to room temperature, then serve.

Brunch is supposed to be easy and fun, so don't get serious with the wines and cocktails.

A personal favorite of mine is a glass of Prosecco with a garnish of fresh strawberry. It's a classic that is tame enough for an early meal. For beer, I opt for a Belgian framboise lambic with its light balance of sweet raspberry and sour tang.

The Monkey Butt

While I tend to favor wine or beer for many events, I truly believe in the cocktail for brunch. For this very reason, I created my brunch time variation of the prohibition-era "Monkey Gland." An absinthe-based drink is just about the most decadent cocktail to enjoy with eggs. It's the kind of beverage that Ernest Hemmingway would have made if he were the bartender at your local greasy spoon.

SERVES 1
ICE CUBES
2 OUNCES GIN
1 OUNCE ORANGE JUICE
1 SPLASH ABSINTHE
1 SPLASH GRENADINE
2 OUNCES SODA WATER

Fill a cocktail shaker one-third full of ice and add the gin, orange juice, absinthe, grenadine, and soda water. Shake for about 15 seconds, strain, and serve over ice in a pint glass.

Ruddy Mary

Have some cheap lager in the refrigerator? Add a shot of tomato juice and a splash of hot sauce, and you have a classic hair-of-the-dog beverage. For more Bloody Mary ideas, refer to the Springtime Brunch Party menu (page 160-162).

SERVES 1
ICE CUBES
12 OUNCE BOTTLE OF CHEAP LAGER, DIVIDED
3 OUNCES TOMATO JUICE
2 DASHES RED HOT SAUCE (ABOUT ¼ TEASPOON)

Fill a cocktail shaker one-third full of ice and add half of the beer, the tomato juice, and the hot sauce. Shake for about 15 seconds and strain into a beer glass. Pour the remaining beer into the glass and serve.

SIMPLE, HEALTHY, & HEARTY

With the lack of farm fresh produce stands, late autumn can be a hard time to eat well. Most of us end up consuming far too much meat, and vegetarians often end up eating far too many cheese pizzas. When the nights are long, and the icy rains start to clatter against the windows, creating a healthful dinner at home can feel like a real chore. It doesn't help that the vegetables from the grocery store often have more in common with a bag of bricks than sustenance. On nights like this, it's just too easy to toss something in the microwave and be done with it.

This menu will change that. There really is nothing more enjoyable than making risotto or a hearty soup while enveloped in an autumn evening. Most importantly, your dinner will be satisfying and healthy. These easy dishes can work together as a meal, or individually as a simple stick-to-the-ribs kind of dinner. The portion size—up to eight from the typical six—allows for leftovers that make fantastic lunches, too.

All of the recipes here are vegetarian, but will also please someone who, like myself, generally prefers tenderloin to tofu. The first trick in cooking vegetarian is to not mimic meat flavors—which is like dressing up a miniature poodle as a wolf for Halloween—but to go in unexpected directions. Too many vegetarian dishes embrace acidic and sweet flavors; an omnivore's palate will find that disconcerting. These dishes exhibit a rounded balance of flavors that will appeal to everyone.

The second trick is to keep a tasty stock on hand that can be frozen into small portion sizes to defrost as needed. Making my Ultimate Veggie Stock (page 000) on the weekend will not only warm up your house with the exotic smell of porcini mushrooms, herbs, and roasted vegetables, but will provide the base for creating delicious meals all week long.

Ultimate Veggie Stock

Since the heart of any cuisine is its sauce, I have created an amazing vegetarian stock that is comparable in depth and flavor to a demi-glace. By focusing on ingredients steeped in umami, this stock renders a deep intensity usually reserved for well-made beef stock. I call for it here in the French Onion Soup (page 95) and the Risotto with Caramelized Shiitake Mushrooms (page 98), but its uses are really endless.

MAKES 2 QUARTS

4 CARROTS, TOPS REMOVED

4 SPANISH ONIONS (ABOUT 4 CUPS), PEELED AND QUARTERED

¼ CUP VEGETABLE OIL

2 CUPS TOMATO PASTE

2 CUPS WHITE WINE

1 OUNCE DRIED PORCINI MUSHROOMS

1 BUNCH CELERY

8 BLACK PEPPERCORNS

2 DRY BAY LEAVES

6 GARLIC CLOVES, PEELED

½ CUP AGED SOY SAUCE

1 TEASPOON SMOKED PAPRIKA

2 TABLESPOONS ROASTED SESAME OIL

Preheat the oven to 400°F. In a large bowl, toss the carrots and onions with oil. Spread them out on a rimmed baking sheet and roast for 35 minutes, turning every 10 minutes, or until very brown. Add the tomato paste to the carrots and onions with a spatula, and roast for another 10 minutes.

Remove the baking sheet from the oven, scoop up the roasted vegetables, and place them in a large stock pot. Pour the white wine onto the baking sheet and scrape up all the roasted bits of vegetables, then add this liquid into the stock pot along with the mushrooms, celery, peppercorns, bay leaves, garlic, soy sauce, paprika, sesame oil, and 1 gallon of water. Bring to a boil then reduce to a simmer for 3 hours. Remove from the heat and let cool for 1 hour.

Strain the stock through a fine mesh strainer into another large stockpot or heatproof container, discarding the solids. Store the stock in sealed containers in the refrigerator for 5 days or in the freezer for up to 4 months.

French Onion Soup

For some reason, my girlfriend thinks that this soup is traditionally vegetarian. It's her favorite, so I don't have the heart to tell her that it's usually made with beef stock. I have adapted the classic recipe to work with the Ultimate Veggie Stock (page 93), which will lend some earthier notes to the dish.

SERVES 8

2 TABLESPOONS EXTRA-VIRGIN OLIVE OIL

6 SPANISH ONIONS (ABOUT 1½ POUNDS), PEELED AND THINLY SLICED

2 DRY BAY LEAVES

½ TEASPOON FINE SALT

½ TEASPOON FRESHLY GROUND BLACK PEPPER

4 GARLIC CLOVES, MINCED

¼ TEASPOON DRIED THYME

¼ TEASPOON DRIED MARJORAM

½ CUP WHITE WINE

8 CUPS ULTIMATE VEGGIE STOCK (PAGE 93)

8 BAGUETTE SLICES, TOASTED

1½ CUPS GRATED GRUYÈRE

¼ CUP GRATED PARMESAN

In a large saucepan over a medium-low flame, heat the oil and sauté the onions and bay leaves until caramelized, about 35 minutes. Add the salt, pepper, garlic, thyme, and marjoram, and sauté for another minute. Add the wine and let the mixture come to a boil, then add the stock. Bring to a boil, and then reduce the sauce to a simmer. Cover the saucepan partially and simmer for 30 minutes. Remove the bay leaves.

Preheat the oven to 375°F. Ladle the soup into eight oven-proof bowls arranged on a sheet pan. Top each with a slice of baguette, ¼ cup Gruyère, and half a tablespoon of Parmesan. Bake in the oven for 10 minutes, or until the cheese starts to brown. Serve immediately.

Panzanella Salad

More crouton than salad, this dish is a perfect way to use stale bread. The preparation also helps to mask the subpar tomatoes generally available during this time of the year.

SERVES 8

1 LOAF DAY-OLD ITALIAN BREAD (ABOUT 1 POUND),
    TORN INTO BITE-SIZE PIECES

⅓ CUP EXTRA-VIRGIN OLIVE OIL

½ TEASPOON FINE SALT

½ TEASPOON FRESHLY GROUND BLACK PEPPER

3 GARLIC CLOVES, MINCED

4 TOMATOES, CUT INTO WEDGES

¾ CUP RED ONION (ABOUT 1 LARGE ONION), SLICED

10 FRESH BASIL LEAVES, SHREDDED

½ CUP GREEN OLIVES, PITTED AND HALVED

1 CUP CHOPPED FRESH MOZZARELLA, CUT INTO BITE-SIZE PIECES

2 TABLESPOONS BALSAMIC VINEGAR

Preheat the oven to 400°F. In a large bowl, toss the bread with the olive oil, salt, pepper, and garlic. Arrange the seasoned bread on a baking sheet and toast for 10 minutes, or until golden in color.

Gently toss together the bread, tomatoes, onion, basil, olives, and mozzarella cheese with the balsamic vinegar. Let rest for 15 minutes before serving.

CORKED & FORKED

Risotto with Caramelized Shiitake Mushrooms

The trick to great risotto is to never add too much liquid at a time, and to keep stirring throughout the cooking process. This method creates a rich floor for the star ingredient, shiitake mushrooms.

SERVES 8

6 CUPS ULTIMATE VEGGIE STOCK (PAGE 93)

3 TABLESPOONS UNSALTED BUTTER

½ POUND FRESH SHIITAKE MUSHROOMS, STEMS REMOVED

2 CUPS ARBORIO RICE

2 SHALLOTS, DICED

1 CUP WHITE WINE

¼ CUP GRATED PARMESAN

In a medium saucepan, bring the stock to a boil, and then reduce to low heat. Keep warm.

In a large sauté pan over medium heat, add the butter. When the butter has melted, add the mushrooms, tops down. Let them cook undisturbed for 5 minutes, or until the tops become deep golden and caramelized. Remove the mushrooms from the pan, slice them into thick strips, and reserve.

Add the rice to the hot pan and toast for 2 minutes, constantly swirling with a spatula. Add the shallots and sauté for another minute, or until translucent. Slowly add the white wine while stirring the rice, until the wine is fully absorbed.

Add the stock in approximately half-cup increments, stirring constantly, and only adding more stock when the previous addition has been completely absorbed. Once the rice is al dente (firm but yielding), after about 15 minutes, stop adding the stock. Remove the risotto from the heat and stir in the mushrooms. Top with the Parmesan just before serving.

BEVERAGE PAIRINGS

This is a red wine dinner from start to finish. For the soup, the classic pairing is Beaujolais. That may be a little shocking: Most people have only tried Beaujolais Nouveau, which tastes like bubblegum. There are many types of Beaujolais, however, most of which don't get much attention outside of France. The best are from certain villages renowned for producing the top grapes. These wines will always have the name of the town on the label. With this soup, I prefer the wines from Régnié, Morgon, and Juliénas.

For the salad, I opt for a Rosso Conero, a blend of the Montepulciano and Sangiovese grapes from the Italian region of Marche. A few Italian barley wines will also make the grade with this salad but I haven't seen them for sale in the States yet. If all else fails, go with a dry rosé.

For the risotto, a Pinotage is a surprisingly excellent pairing, especially one from the Paarl region of South Africa, as it highlights the mushroom flavors infused in the rice. A Belgian-style American beer is a great pairing, too. In fact, it's a better match for this than authentic Belgian ale because brewers in the U.S. use more of a certain type of yeast—known as brett—that lends their beers a more intense earthiness than their Belgian counterparts.

WINTER

THE COLD IS SETTLING IN AND THE DAYS ARE GROWING CONSPICUOUSLY SHORTER. There will be days, weeks, maybe even months where sunshine will become a rare sight, rarer than a unicorn playing jazz on a harpsichord. Somewhere along the line, winter seems to become an infinite expanse of gray.

BUT THIS GRAY SEASON IS ALSO WHEN PEOPLE CAN BE AT THEIR BEST. Even in the most hurried cities the pace of our lives slows down. The blare of the horns peter out and tranquility descends, as long as you stay out of the shopping malls come December.

THIS IS THE TIME OF YEAR WHEN DINNER PARTIES AND CELEBRATIONS MATTER MOST. There are the big religious holidays, of course, and the romance of Valentine's Day. But there is much more. THE LONG EXPANSE OF DREARY WEEKS CAN BE FILLED WITH LAUGHTER, GENEROSITY, AND JOVIALITY. Truthfully, I have always found that winter parties make the best celebrations.

Filling a house with warmth and the scents of good food is inherently redemptive and reinvigorating. Those summertime anxieties of bathing suits are long gone, replaced with layers of clothing and the biological need to stay warm. It's the time of year when very little surpasses the pleasure of a home-cooked meal. THIS IS THE SEASON WHERE YOUR EFFORTS IN THE KITCHEN WILL BE MOST APPRECIATED BY FRIENDS AND FAMILY; THIS IS THE COOK'S TIME TO SHINE.

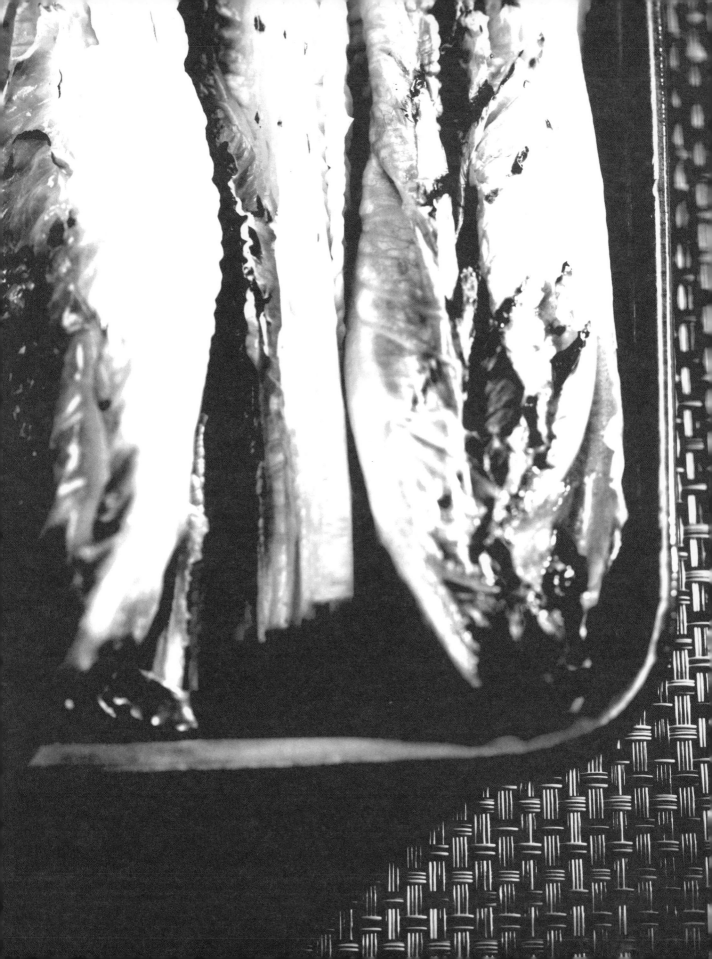

FAMILY HOLIDAY DINNER

There is a point between childhood and adulthood when giving gifts becomes more important than getting gifts, that time when the holidays move beyond the magical realm of Saint Nick to something more elemental, where being the agent of happiness taps into something quite profound.

One of the greatest gifts is to give your time, labor, and imagination in the preparation of a family holiday dinner. I know from experience that it's all too easy to get distracted by family peccadilloes. These are people you know all too well, and no doubt there will be a slew of culinary phobias to reckon with.

My suggestion is to plan the entire event conservatively. When planning the menu, offer up dishes that are recognizable classics. We will add an intriguing edge to the meal by reaching back a century or two to reconstruct some traditional recipes for the modern palate. To your guests, eating these transformed dishes will be like sitting in center orchestra seats at the symphony after a lifetime of listening to classical music on the radio.

By serving your family well-known dishes, you have let them stay in their comfort zone. By preparing those foods in an exciting and classic way, you have given their taste buds a jumpstart. And plying them with perhaps a bit more alcohol than they are used to, well, that can't hurt, either.

Grilled Caesar Salad

In these chapters I've encouraged you to take some culinary risks in the kitchen; don't be afraid to take them tableside as well. This dish makes for a grand display when prepared in front of guests. Of course, you should practice it a few times beforehand so that the presentation appears flawless and professional. It will also allow you to garnish the salad to the specifications of each guest.

SERVES 4

2 SMALL GARLIC CLOVES, MINCED

2 ANCHOVY FILLETS, MINCED (OR ½ TEASPOON ANCHOVY PASTE)

1 EGG

2 TABLESPOONS FRESHLY SQUEEZED LEMON JUICE (ABOUT 1 LARGE LEMON)

1 TABLESPOON DIJON MUSTARD

¼ TEASPOON WORCESTERSHIRE SAUCE

¾ CUP EXTRA-VIRGIN OLIVE OIL, DIVIDED

½ TEASPOON KOSHER SALT

½ TEASPOON FRESHLY GROUND BLACK PEPPER

2 HEADS ROMAINE, CUT IN HALF LENGTHWISE

½ CUP PARMESAN, SHAVED

In a small bowl, whisk together the garlic, anchovies, egg, lemon juice, mustard, and Worcestershire. Add ½ cup of olive oil to the mixture in a stream, whisking until the dressing is emulsified. Season with the salt and the pepper. Refrigerate until ready to serve.

Preheat your grill to medium-high heat. Remove any dark green or damaged romaine leaves. Brush the remaining oil over the cut edges of the romaine. Place the lettuce cut-side down and grill for 2 minutes. Turn and grill for 1 more minute, or until grill marks form on the leaves. Remove from the grill and let sit.

In a large salad bowl, add ½ head of romaine for each serving, and dress the salad according to taste (using about 1 ounce of dressing per serving, plus more or less as desired). Plate the lettuce grilled-side up and sprinkle with the Parmesan before serving.

Alternatively, to prepare the salad tableside, arrange the grilled romaine, along with the ingredients for the dressing, on a small table close to the guests. Whisk together the dressing just before serving, then plate and dress each salad according to taste, followed by a sprinkling of Parmesan.

Oysta Rockafella

The original recipe from the nineteenth century is still a well-guarded secret. However, with a little help from my friends in Louisiana, this preparation is the closest to the real deal as you will ever get. For the oysters, I strongly suggest purchasing from a grocer or a fishmonger who will shuck them for you in advance.

SERVES 4 TO 6

2 DOZEN OYSTERS, SHUCKED, ON THE HALF SHELL

8 SPRIGS ITALIAN PARSLEY

4 SCALLIONS (WHITE AND GREEN PARTS), DICED

½ CUP FRESH CELERY LEAVES (ABOUT 3 STALKS), ROUGHLY CHOPPED

8 FRESH TARRAGON LEAVES

1 TEASPOON DRY CHERVIL LEAVES

1 TABLESPOON CAPERS

4 TABLESPOONS EXTRA-VIRGIN OLIVE OIL

½ CUP DRIED BREAD CRUMBS

1 STICK (½ CUP) UNSALTED BUTTER, SOFTENED

½ TEASPOON KOSHER SALT

½ TEASPOON FRESHLY GROUND BLACK PEPPER

1 TEASPOON HOT SAUCE

2 TABLESPOONS ABSINTHE

Preheat the oven to 450°F. In a food processor, purée the parsley, scallions, celery leaves, tarragon, chervil, capers, olive oil, bread crumbs, butter, salt, pepper, hot sauce, and absinthe until the mixture turns creamy-smooth. Ladle evenly onto the shucked oysters, and set the shell halves on a baking sheet. Bake for 6 minutes or until the oyster flesh is bouncy to the touch. Serve immediately.

Braised Lamb Shank with Herbes de Provence

A perfect holiday entrée: rich, savory, and impressive. An added benefit is that this dish can be prepared a day or two in advance, and in fact, the shank will only taste better the longer it sits in its braising liquid. One note of caution: Make sure to minimize the exposure of the lamb to air during the cooking process, as it will quickly toughen the meat.

SERVES 6

6 LAMB SHANKS

½ TEASPOON KOSHER SALT

½ TEASPOON FRESHLY GROUND BLACK PEPPER

2 TABLESPOONS EXTRA-VIRGIN OLIVE OIL

2 SPANISH ONIONS (ABOUT 2 CUPS), CHOPPED

3 LARGE CARROTS (ABOUT 2 CUPS), PEELED AND CUT INTO ¼-INCH ROUNDS

10 GARLIC CLOVES, MINCED

1 BOTTLE RED WINE, PREFERABLY A CÔTES DU RHÔNE

1 (28-OUNCE) CAN CRUSHED TOMATOES, WITH JUICE

2 (10.5-OUNCE) CANS BEEF STOCK

2 TEASPOONS DRIED ROSEMARY

1 TEASPOON DRIED HERBES DE PROVENCE

Sprinkle shanks with salt and pepper. Heat the oil in a heavy, large pot over medium-high heat. Working in batches, cook the shanks until they turn brown on both sides, about 4 minutes per side. Transfer shanks to a plate and set aside.

Add the onions, carrots, and garlic to the cooking pot and sauté until golden-brown, about 10 minutes. Stir in the wine, tomatoes, and stock and let boil for 5 minutes. Add the herbes de Provence and the rosemary to the sauce. Return the shanks to the pot, pressing down firmly to submerge them in the stock. Bring back to a boil for 3 minutes, then reduce heat to medium-low. Cover and simmer on medium-low heat until meat is tender, about 2 hours.

Remove the lamb, and simmer the sauce about 20 minutes longer on medium-low heat until the sauce has thickened. Return the lamb to the sauce and simmer for another 10 minutes. You can serve immediately, or store in the refrigerator for one or two days. To reheat, return the lamb and the sauce to a pot and reheat over medium heat. Let it simmer slowly for 7 minutes before serving.

Spicy Chocolate and Gingersnap Tart

Chile and chocolate is a classic Mexican flavor combination, but has only recently found its way into mainstream desserts. This recipe is a great riff on the classic chocolate tart. It can be made a day in advance, provided it is tightly sealed and refrigerated, then brought to room temperature before serving.

SERVES 12

Crust

8 OUNCES GINGERSNAP COOKIES (ABOUT 32 COOKIES), COARSELY BROKEN

½ STICK (¼ CUP) UNSALTED BUTTER, MELTED

PINCH OF FINE SALT

Filling

12 OUNCES BITTERSWEET CHOCOLATE, FINELY CHOPPED

1 CUP HEAVY WHIPPING CREAM

2 LARGE EGG YOLKS

1 LARGE EGG

¼ CUP GRANULATED SUGAR

1 TABLESPOON ALL-PURPOSE FLOUR

⅛ TEASPOON FRESHLY GROUND BLACK PEPPER

1 TEASPOON GROUND CINNAMON

¼ TEASPOON FINE SALT

⅛ TEASPOON CAYENNE PEPPER

2 TABLESPOONS CRYSTALLIZED GINGER, COARSELY CHOPPED

Preheat oven to 325°F.

For the crust: Finely grind the gingersnap cookies in a food processor (yielding 1½ to 1⅔ cups of crumbs). Add the melted butter and salt to the mixture, and process until moistened. Press the crumb mixture firmly onto the entire surface of 9-inch-diameter tart pan with a removable bottom. Place the pan on a rimmed baking sheet.

For the chocolate filling: Combine the finely chopped bittersweet chocolate and heavy whipping cream in a heavy, medium-sized sauté pan. Whisk over low heat until the chocolate becomes melted and smooth, about 4 minutes. Remove the pan from the heat. In a medium-sized bowl, whisk the egg yolks, egg, sugar, flour, black pepper, cinnamon, salt, and cayenne pepper until blended. Very gradually whisk the chocolate mixture into the egg mixture until smooth. Pour the chocolate filling into the crust.

Bake the chocolate tart until the filling puffs slightly at its edges and the center is softly set, about 30 minutes. Transfer to a cooling rack. Sprinkle the chopped crystallized ginger over the top of the tart. Cool the tart in its pan for 20 minutes. Gently remove the sides of the tart pan and let cool completely to room temperature.

Cut tart into thin wedges and serve.

BEVERAGE PAIRINGS

This Caesar is richer than most salads, so the best wine pairing will be a white Burgundy. Specifically, a Rully Premier Cru will offer a touch of savoriness alongside a lush edge of cream. For a beer pairing, a Czech Pilsner will play off the Parmesan flavors and echo the crispness of the romaine in a deeply satisfying way.

For the Oysta Rockafella, you can stay with the white Burgundy for wine, which layers on the butteriness in a decadent manner. However, a great pairing that will surprise your guests is a stout with the oysters; it draws out a spectacular sweetness from the dish.

For the lamb, go with one of the greatest wines produced in America: a Pinot Noir from the Eola-Amity Hills region of the Willamette Valley in Oregon. The pairing is so beautiful that your tongue may sprout wings and fly to heaven. An American stout will do as well, although the pairing won't be as dramatic.

For the chocolate tart the American stout is in fact the best match: it will add extra dimensions to the chocolate and smooth out the chile spice. A Port-style dessert wine made from Zinfandel grapes will also provide a fine accompaniment to the dessert, and is an ideal way to end any family meal.

TEN-MINUTE FEAST

Preparing a meal in ten minutes with whatever ingredients happen to be on hand is the Holy Grail for home cooks. However, this is actually the method generally used by professional chefs. What folks often don't realize is that restaurant food is very straightforward—it has to be. A professional cook typically has less than ten minutes to prepare a dish while cooking upwards of twenty orders at a time. The most difficult part of restaurant cooking is juggling so much food and having each dish come out exactly right.

The main difference for the home cook is that a professional maintains stations of prepared ingredients, ranging from tomato *concassé* to *demi-glace*, at their fingertips. At home, of course, it's a completely different scenario. The trick is to employ some shortcuts, such as using frozen vegetables or presoaked beans, when assembling a quick meal made from items already in the pantry.

Despite running a wine school for a living and writing cookbooks for fun, I like to think that I am a realist. Sure, making healthy meals from fresh and local ingredients is a great and noble cause (of course I would say that!) but the truth is that we don't always have the time to do it on a daily basis. To be perfectly honest, there have been many days while working on this book when I opted to grab pizza instead of making lunch or dinner. Those desperate moments were the inspiration for the following dishes.

This chapter is about the simple meal, the kind you can make in a brief period of time at home without having any special ingredients on hand. I added some fancy names to hide the fact that these recipes are so uncomplicated. Yet another tried-and-true restaurant trick.

Calabacín Español (Spanish Zucchini)

This dish is inspired by the flavors of Northern Spain. The bitterness of the zucchini plays off the sweetness of the roasted pepper, and the anchovy and olives bring a necessary brininess to the equation.

SERVES 6

1 TABLESPOON EXTRA-VIRGIN OLIVE OIL

1 TEASPOON RED PEPPER FLAKES

1 ANCHOVY FILLET, CHOPPED

1 GARLIC CLOVE, MINCED

1 SPANISH ONION (ABOUT 1 CUP), DICED

1 (12-OUNCE) JAR FIRE-ROASTED PEPPERS, DRAINED AND CHOPPED

½ CUP BLACK OLIVES, PITTED

2 MEDIUM ZUCCHINI (ABOUT 12 OUNCES), SLICED ½-INCH-THICK ON THE BIAS

Set a sauté pan over medium-high heat and add the oil. When the oil is hot, add the pepper flakes and anchovies. Let the anchovies disintegrate, about 1 minute. Add the garlic and gently brown, then add the onions and sauté until translucent, about 2 to 3 minutes. Toss in the roasted peppers and black olives. Sauté for 3 minutes until fragrant. Finally, add the zucchini and sauté until lightly brown at the edges, about 2 minutes. Remove from heat and serve immediately.

Supreme de Volaille avec la Sauce de Trois Fromages ("Chicken with Cheese Sauce")

This is one of those dishes that unites pretty much everyone. Who doesn't love chicken and cheese? The trick with this dish is to stir the sauce as soon as you add the flour so that it doesn't get lumpy. For both the Brie and the cheddar, you can substitute any other cheese on hand.

SERVES 6

2 BONELESS, SKINLESS CHICKEN BREASTS

½ TEASPOON KOSHER SALT

½ TEASPOON FRESHLY GROUND BLACK PEPPER

2 TABLESPOONS VEGETABLE OIL

1 STICK UNSALTED BUTTER

½ CUP ALL-PURPOSE FLOUR

1 PINT HEAVY CREAM

2 OUNCES BRIE, ROUGHLY CHOPPED

2 OUNCES AGED CHEDDAR, ROUGHLY CHOPPED

¼ CUP GRATED PARMESAN

Preheat the oven to 375°F. In a large bowl, coat the chicken breasts with the salt, pepper, and oil. Set a large ovenproof sauté pan over medium heat and sear the breasts for 7 minutes on each side, or until lightly browned. Transfer the pan to the oven for about 10 minutes, or until an instant-read thermometer reads 170°F. Remove the chicken from the oven, and let it rest on a cutting board.

Meanwhile, return the sauté pan to a burner set at medium heat. Add the butter to the pan. Once it's melted, add the flour and whisk to combine. Cook the roux for 2 minutes, whisking slowly, or until it thickens and the flour smells toasty. Continue whisking while slowly, and carefully, adding the cream. Cook for 2 more minutes, then add the cheeses. Gently whisk until the mixture is velvety in texture.

Slice the chicken into medallions, and dress with 2 ounces of sauce on each plate. Serve.

Minestrone de Six Minutes ("Speedy Minestrone")

This may be the fastest meal ever. I received a number of funny looks when I first made this dish, and you will, too. But don't worry; your guests will stop questioning your sanity as soon as they taste it.

SERVES 6

¼ CUP **EXTRA-VIRGIN OLIVE OIL**

2 **CLOVES GARLIC, MINCED**

1 **TEASPOON CRUSHED RED PEPPER FLAKES**

1 **SPANISH ONION (ABOUT 1 CUP), CHOPPED**

1 **(14-OUNCE) CAN CANNELLINI BEANS, RINSED AND DRAINED**

1 **(14-OUNCE) CAN DICED TOMATOES**

16 **OUNCES LOW-SODIUM VEGETABLE JUICE (SUCH AS V8)**

½ **TEASPOON FINE SALT**

½ **TEASPOON FRESHLY GROUND BLACK PEPPER**

Add the olive oil to a stock pot over medium-high heat. Once hot, toss in the garlic and hot pepper flakes, and sauté until the garlic is lightly browned, about 1 minute. Add the onions and sauté until translucent, about 2 to 3 minutes.

Add the beans and tomatoes, and bring to a simmer. Reduce the heat to medium and simmer for 2 minutes. Add the vegetable juice, and simmer for 3 minutes. Add the salt and pepper, and serve.

Yiaourti me Meli ("Yogurt with Honey")

Greek yogurt, which is much denser and more velvety than most yogurts, is the star of the show. If you have it, a chestnut honey will take this dish to the next level. Otherwise, all-natural and organic plain yogurt, along with the ubiquitous honey bear, will do.

SERVES 6

1 TABLESPOON HONEY
1 CUP PLAIN GREEK YOGURT
1 TABLESPOON WALNUT PIECES
2 CUPS SEASONAL FRUIT

In a medium bowl, stir together the honey, yogurt, and walnuts. Pour over the fruit, and enjoy! (Really, that's it.)

BEVERAGE PAIRINGS

Initially I sketched out a number of very specific wine pairings with this meal. An Aglianico with the minestrone, a Xarel-lo with the zucchini, and a Prosecco di Conegliano Valdobbiadene with the chicken. But why go out of your way to find some obscure wines for a meal you are whipping up with stuff from your pantry and refrigerator? That would be silly.

Instead, I'll suggest a simple rule: keep away from white Zinfandel and anything with a cartoon animal on it. Anything else will be just fine for this quick and easy fare.

The real pairing lesson that can be learned here is to always have a cache of decent and inexpensive wines at home, beverages that you can enjoy any time or any day, with any meal. Right now, my favorite everyday red wines are Côtes du Rhônes from France and Riojas crianza from Spain. For whites, I keep a few Austrian Rieslings and an Australian Marsanne on hand. However, all that will likely change in a month or so, because the best part of keeping an inexpensive wine collection at home is to change it up frequently. For a beer, the only way to go is with a winter seasonal beer. Pretty much every microbrewery creates its own version, so go with your local favorite.

WINTERTIME HOUSE PARTY

One of the best times to throw an unabashed house party is during February, the dark heart of the winter season. I'm not talking five or six folks; I envision dozens of friends converging for a great big hopping damn-the-carpets, who's-that-passed-out-in-the-garage type of party. As the host, an event of this magnitude can be overwhelming. It's still worth the effort, and I'll explain why.

First, take a step back for a moment. A great party should be like a wildfire of joy. From the moment the front door opens, a spark is ignited. Soon after, an explosion of laughter cracks open social boundaries and all bets are off. The shy, goofy guy rises to the status of armchair celebrity. The aloof doctor is telling off-color jokes to a cherubic seminarian. A restaurant critic is singing the praises of pork rinds to a bemused house painter. And that is only in the first hour.

To allow your party to reach that perfect fever pitch, you have to think through every nitty-gritty detail in advance. When planning the menu, it's best to serve single tapas-sized portions of food on large trays, and to never serve anything that requires a spoon or a knife. Additionally, keep cleanup to a minimum. If you are going to host more than fifteen people at your party, use recyclable plates and dining ware exclusively, and keep plenty of small recycling and trash bins placed strategically throughout your home. Stack large paper napkins in every room just in case there is a spill. You will find that your guests will pretty much clean up after themselves when the right tools are at hand.

The recipes I have created for this party are rich and hearty. They make twenty portions for guests; for a smaller party, simply reduce the quantities for fewer servings. The dishes should all be made at least one day ahead of time. That way, you can focus on your job for the night: enjoying an evening filled with raucous laughter and the appreciation of your friends.

Three Pigs and a Duck Soup

This is the soup you will want to eat every blustery night, so share it with your guests. It takes two different types of porky goodness—pancetta and bacon—and adds a third: the duck stock is flavored with a ham hock. It can be made one or two days ahead of time.

SERVES 20

1 POUND (½ CUP) SMOKED BACON, DICED

1 SMALL SPANISH ONION (ABOUT ½ CUP), DICED

4 CUPS DUCK STOCK (PAGE 64)

6 RUSSET POTATOES, DICED (ABOUT 3 CUPS)

1 POUND PANCETTA, DICED (ABOUT ½ CUP)

1 MEDIUM CARROT, DICED (ABOUT ½ CUP)

3 CELERY STALKS, DICED (ABOUT ½ CUP)

½ TEASPOON FINE SALT

½ TEASPOON FRESHLY GROUND BLACK PEPPER

Set a large stock pot over medium-low heat and add the bacon. When the bacon has begun to crisp and has rendered much of its fat, add the onion. Cook until the onion turns translucent, about 2 to 3 minutes.

Add the duck stock, potatoes, pancetta, carrot, and celery, and bring to a boil. Reduce to a simmer, and cook for 15 minutes. Add the salt and pepper. Blend with an immersion blender in the pot, or carefully transfer to a blender and purée in batches.

Ladle into small, insulated paper cups and serve.

Portuguese Duck Rice

I think ducks migrate south because they know how tasty they are. Personally, I wouldn't hang around either if I had a reputation as being such a delicious wintertime snack. This recipe makes the best of the duck's fatty and flavorful qualities, and stretches out a single duck into tapas-sized snacks for twenty people.

SERVES 20

1 (3 TO 5 POUND) DUCK, FRESH OR THAWED

4 GARLIC CLOVES

2 SPANISH ONIONS (ABOUT 2 CUPS), CHOPPED

½ LEMON

1 TEASPOON DRIED THYME

1 TEASPOON DRIED MARJORAM

1 DRIED BAY LEAF

1 SMOKED HAM HOCK (ABOUT 8 TO 12 OUNCES)

4 OUNCES BACON (ABOUT ¼ CUP), DICED

1 POUND LONG-GRAIN WHITE RICE

Place the duck in a large stock pot with the garlic, onion, lemon, thyme, marjoram, bay leaf, ham hock, and bacon. Cover with water (at least 9 cups) and bring to a boil. Reduce the heat to low, and keep at a low simmer for 1 hour, skimming fat every 10 minutes. Let cool for 30 minutes and then refrigerate for at least 3 hours. Remove the bay leaf and the lemon. Skim any fat off the surface of the stock; remove the duck and set aside. Strain the stock and reserve.

In a medium saucepan, add 5 cups of the duck stock to the rice. Bring to a boil for 1 minute, then cover tightly and turn off the heat. Let stand for about 15 minutes. The rice should be slightly undercooked, with liquid remaining in the pan.

Pull the skin, fat, and meat off of the duck and shred together.

Pour the rice into a 13 x 9-inch baking dish, and add the duck meat and fat mixture in a layer over the rice. Let cool and store, covered, in the refrigerator overnight; this will help intensify the flavors.

When ready to serve, preheat the oven to 350°F. Bake the rice casserole uncovered for about 25 minutes, until the rice is fully cooked, the stock has been absorbed, and the duck is crisp. For a crowd, serve in small paper bowls with disposable wooden forks.

Roasted Butternut Squash with Sage and Parmesan

It's the perfect time of year for the sweetest of squashes. Roasting amplifies their flavor, and adding a bit of sage and Parmesan lends a few more layers of savory depth.

SERVES 20

2 STICKS (1 CUP) UNSALTED BUTTER

1 TABLESPOON FINE SALT

¼ CUP LIGHT BROWN SUGAR, LOOSELY PACKED

3 WHOLE BUTTERNUT SQUASHES (ABOUT 9 POUNDS), PEELED AND CUT INTO 1-INCH CUBES

2 TABLESPOONS DRIED SAGE

¾ CUP SHAVED PARMESAN

Preheat the oven and two baking sheets to 400°F. In a large pot, melt the butter over medium heat. Add the salt and sugar. Then add the squash and sage, and mix to coat evenly.

Using an oven mitt, remove the sheet trays from the oven. Carefully spread the squash evenly over the sheet trays and bake for 10 minutes. Remove from the oven, and using a spatula, turn the squash pieces over as best as you can. Return the sheets to the oven for another 15 minutes, or until the squash is lightly golden at the edges and cooked through. Remove from the oven. If preparing a day in advance, allow the squash to cool, then refrigerate. To reheat, warm in a 200°F oven for 10 minutes before your guests arrive.

Place a toothpick into each piece of squash, garnish with Parmesan, and serve on a large tray.

Rosemary Cookies

These shortbread cookies flavored with rosemary close the party on a high note. Unlike most desserts, they will pair nicely with both wine and beer owing to their sweet and savory flavors.

MAKES 40 COOKIES

3 STICKS (1½ CUPS) UNSALTED BUTTER, AT ROOM TEMPERATURE,
    PLUS MORE FOR GREASING PANS
⅔ CUP CONFECTIONERS' SUGAR
2¾ CUPS ALL-PURPOSE FLOUR, PLUS MORE FOR DUSTING
¼ TEASPOON FINE SALT
1½ TABLESPOONS DRIED ROSEMARY, FINELY CHOPPED

In a large bowl, beat the butter with the confectioners' sugar until fluffy, about 5 minutes. Blend in the flour, salt, and rosemary to form a thick dough. Form into a ball and knead for about 2 minutes, or until the dough feels soft and pliable. Shape into a disc, wrap well in plastic, and refrigerate for 2 hours until firm.

Preheat the oven to 300°F. Grease two or three large baking sheets with additional butter.

Lightly flour a large cutting board or work surface and roll out the ball of dough with a rolling pin to about ¼-inch thickness. Cut into 2 x 2-inch squares and place 1 inch apart on the greased baking sheet. Bake for 20 minutes, or until golden-brown. Cool completely on a wire rack before serving.

BEVERAGE PAIRINGS

Parties are not about elaborate wines and spirits. They are about gossip, off-color jokes, and generally bad behavior. Sure, guests may be talking about your food for months afterward, but they will also be laughing about the time Tom put the moves on a hot little cross-dresser named Robin (all too true of a story).

You want plenty of booze at a party. There should be a dozen bottles of wine, at least one for every four guests, and twice as much beer. As the host, walk through the party with a bottle in one hand and a glass in the other, pouring intoxicants and chatting up guests. Make the atmosphere one of an over the top bacchanalia. But the reverse is actually true: you are controlling everyone's alcohol intake. The last thing you want in your home is drunken bedlam.

This is a trick I learned from running hundreds of events at both the Wine School and the Beer School. Keeping everyone happy, but not drunk, is all in the choice of beverages and the size of your glassware. The first rule is to never serve hard alcohol, at least at a wintertime party. The second is to locate all of the drinks in one spot; it's easier to keep an eye on consumption and creates a natural bottleneck. Finally, use small, stemmed glassware (or plastic ware). People drink about half as fast when they are sipping from an eight-ounce glass rather than the more typical sixteen-ounce glass.

Your choice for beer and wine is important, too. Beers should be Czech lagers and rich, malty stouts, because they are low in alcohol. If you want to have another choice, lay your hands on some IPAs (India pale ales): these are ideal sipping beers. Keep away from Belgian styles, however, because they are too high in alcohol and far too easy to drink.

Wine is a bit trickier. Most selections from California and Australia these days are obscenely high in alcohol. Someone might end up in a snow bank. Your best bets, then, are inexpensive sparkling wines, such as a Crémant from France or a Cava from Spain. Sparkling wines are not only festive, but are meant to be sipped. For reds, I go for a Dolcetto d'Alba from Italy or a Chinon from France, both of which are delicious, but too earthy in flavor to drink quickly. Whatever you choose, make sure to keep the alcohol content under thirteen percent.

THE RETRO DINNER PARTY

I t's time to hit the vintage stores and pull out the monogrammed aprons: this is the season for a retro dinner party. Winter's been going on so long now that you really need to stir it up a bit. A fifties theme is perfect, since it combines the fun of a costume party with the style of a dinner party.

Mid-century America was all about the swank. The swooping lines of a '59 Lincoln Towncar, the modernist skyscrapers like the Seagram Building, gleaming and functional, gentlemen sporting dapper suits and fedoras, and ladies in smart dresses accented with piping and pearls.

It was an era of high style, except for the food. If it wasn't flavorless and fried, then it was boiled, buttered, and gray. It was the cuisine of WASP-y families across New England, and probably all of America at the time. (If you ever wonder why those Boston Brahmins never smile, it's not that they don't like you—it's chronic indigestion.)

To make the food interesting, I took a selection of my least favorite mid-century dishes and deconstructed them. I separated the taste spark in each—that little bit of flavor that evokes a guilty pleasure—and rebuilt the dish around that element, tossing out the rest. The resulting dishes are refreshingly modern, but make a knowing reference back to the good ole days. As you will find, nothing banishes the winter blues like a night of classic style.

Crudités Shots with Shallot Purée

The flavors of crudités with French onion dip are recreated here in a fun and playful "shot" format. It's essential that the shallots in the purée are caramelized, so pay extra-careful attention to their browning during the cooking process. This dish is best served at room temperature, or just barely warmed.

SERVES 6

Carrot and Cucumber Shot

1 TABLESPOON UNSALTED BUTTER

1 TEASPOON FINE SALT

1 TEASPOON WHITE PEPPER

1 SMALL SPANISH ONION (ABOUT ½ CUP), DICED

1½ CUPS VEGETABLE OR CHICKEN STOCK

2 MEDIUM CARROTS, PEELED AND ROUGHLY CHOPPED (ABOUT 1 CUP)

1 SMALL CUCUMBER, PEELED AND ROUGHLY CHOPPED

1 CUP HEAVY WHIPPING CREAM

Caramelized Shallot Purée

2 TEASPOONS UNSALTED BUTTER

3 SHALLOTS, SLICED

2 CUPS WHITE WINE

2 TABLESPOONS SOUR CREAM

1 TEASPOON EXTRA-VIRGIN OLIVE OIL

¼ TEASPOON PAPRIKA

For the shot: In a 6-quart pan over medium-high heat, add the butter, salt, white pepper, and onions and cook, stirring often, until the onions turn translucent, about 2 to 3 minutes. Add the stock and the carrots. Cover and bring to a boil. Reduce heat and simmer for 9 minutes, or until the carrots are tender. Add the cucumbers, stir once, and remove from heat immediately.

Once the mixture is cool enough to handle, transfer to a food processor. Pulse until the mixture turns to a soup-like consistency. Return to the pan and add the cream, stirring over a high heat until boiling. Remove from heat and run through a fine sieve. Set aside.

For the purée: In a small sauté pan over medium-high heat, add the butter. Once the butter just begins to smoke, add the shallots and stir until deep brown, about 4 minutes. Add the white wine and let boil for 4 minutes, or until the sauce has slightly thickened. Reduce the temperature to medium and let simmer for another 4 minutes, or until the sauce is as thick as heavy cream. Transfer to a food processor and pulse 3 times, or until thoroughly blended. Mix in the sour cream. Run the mixture through a fine sieve and set aside.

To serve, ladle 2 ounces (about 4 tablespoons) of the carrot and cucumber mixture into six large shot glasses, drizzle 1 teaspoon of the purée on the top of each, and finish with one drop of olive oil and a sprinkle of paprika before serving.

Caramelized Mushrooms with Scallop Sausage

This old sawhorse of a recipe is found on the menus of country clubs everywhere. I've changed it up by using higher-quality mushrooms and baking them with a scallop mousse flavored by traditional sausage herbs. The textures are wonderful, as is the balance between the sweetness of the scallop and the earthiness of the mushroom.

SERVES 4 TO 6

2 TABLESPOONS EXTRA-VIRGIN OLIVE OIL

20 CRIMINI MUSHROOM CAPS

8 OUNCES SEA SCALLOPS, MUSCLE REMOVED, RINSED AND PATTED DRY

1 EGG WHITE

1 TEASPOON GARLIC SALT

¼ TEASPOON WHITE PEPPER

¼ TEASPOON ANISE

¼ TEASPOON GROUND MACE

¼ CUP VERY COLD HEAVY WHIPPING CREAM

Preheat the oven to 425°F. Brush the tops and bottoms of the mushroom caps with the olive oil. Place on a baking sheet and roast in the oven, cap-side up for 10 minutes, or until the gills start to brown and caramelize. Flip the caps over and caramelize the other side, about 10 minutes.

Place the scallops into the bowl of a food processor and pulse 5 to 6 times, until puréed. Add the egg white and pulse 2 more times, or until the mixture is thoroughly combined. Scrape down the sides of the mixing bowl and add the garlic salt, pepper, anise, and mace. Pulse to incorporate all of the ingredients. With the food processor running, slowly add the cold heavy cream. Scrape down the sides of the bowl one last time, and pulse for 5 more seconds, until the mixture becomes the consistency of pudding.

Remove the mushroom caps from the oven and reduce the oven temperature to 350°F. Allow the mushrooms to cool enough to handle safely. Place the mousse into a pastry bag (or a resealable plastic bag with a corner snipped off) and pipe equal amounts of the mousse into each mushroom cap. Bake for another 10 minutes. Plate and serve immediately.

Goat Cheese Log

The infamous cheese log is pretty much the lowest point of culinary preparations: any recipe that calls for a "cheese product" instead of cheese should be avoided like the plague. To reclaim this recipe, we use a log of Bûcheron, which is a classic style of goat cheese in the shape of a log.

SERVES 12

1 BÛCHERON LOG (ABOUT 3 POUNDS),
   OR A LARGE LOG OF GOAT CHEESE
8 OUNCES PINE NUTS, ROASTED
½ CUP DRIED CRANBERRIES
½ CUP DRIED FIGS, DICED

Remove the cheese from its wrapper and pat dry. Cover the bottom of a sheet tray, with the pine nuts, cranberries, and figs, and blend thoroughly. Gently lift the cheese and roll it over the mixture, making sure to press hard enough to embed all of the fruit and nut pieces into the outer layer of the cheese. Place on a serving platter and refrigerate until ready to serve.

CORKED & FORKED

Belgian Beef with Porcini Mushrooms and Egg Noodles

This is my adaptation of beef stroganoff as prepared in mid-century America. The most important step is to reserve enough braising liquid to serve at least one-half cup of sauce with each entrée. If necessary, you can dilute the remaining juices with hot water or heavy cream to yield enough sauce.

SERVES 4 TO 6

6 SLICES THICK-CUT BACON, CHOPPED (ABOUT 1 CUP)

3 TO 4 POUNDS BEEF CHUCK ROAST, FAT TRIMMED

2 LARGE SPANISH ONIONS (ABOUT 2½ CUPS), COARSELY CHOPPED

4 LARGE GARLIC CLOVES, THINLY SLICED

2 BAY LEAVES

1 OUNCE (ABOUT 1 CUP) DRIED PORCINI MUSHROOMS

2 TABLESPOONS TOMATO PASTE

2 LARGE CARROTS, CUT INTO 1-INCH PIECES

1 TABLESPOON FRESHLY GROUND BLACK PEPPER

2 BOTTLES (750 ML) BELGIAN TRIPEL ALE

1 POUND EGG NOODLES, COOKED ACCORDING TO PACKAGE DIRECTIONS

Preheat the oven to 300°F. Lay the bacon in a deep, heavy casserole pan and cook in the oven for 20 minutes, or until the bacon turns very crispy. Remove the bacon and reserve, leaving the fat in the pan. Place the beef into the pan with the bacon fat, being mindful of spattering fat from the pan. Return the pan to the oven. Bake for 15 minutes, or until well-browned. Turn 90 degrees and roast for another 15 minutes.

Remove the pan from the oven and add the onions, garlic, bay leaves, porcini mushrooms, tomato paste, carrots, pepper, and bacon to the pan, stirring to coat everything with bacon fat. Cook for another 5 minutes, or until the onions start to caramelize against the bottom of the pan. Pour in the beer with 4 cups of water, and cover the pan. Return to the oven and roast for 2 hours, turning the meat once halfway through, or until a fork goes into the beef like butter.

Remove the beef to a cutting board, and let it rest for 10 minutes.

Slice the meat into servings, distribute among bowls along with a serving of egg noodles, and ladle a half cup of the sauce over each serving. Serve immediately.

English Chocolate Pudding with Hard Sauce

This dessert is an English classic. The contrasts of bitter and sweet in this pudding are scandalous, and electrically delicious. The key step is to seal the bowl tightly so that the pudding does not turn soggy while cooking.

SERVES 4 TO 6

Pudding

½ TEASPOON BAKING SODA

½ CUP HOT WATER

1 CUP PLUS ½ TABLESPOON GRANULATED SUGAR, DIVIDED

½ CUP UNSULPHURED BLACKSTRAP MOLASSES

¼ CUP DUTCH COCOA

½ CUP DRIED DATES, DICED

1½ CUPS SELF-RISING FLOUR

Hard Sauce

½ CUP UNSALTED BUTTER

½ CUP HEAVY CREAM

1 TEASPOON VANILLA EXTRACT

In a large mixing bowl, dissolve the baking soda in the hot water. Stir in ½ tablespoon of the sugar and the molasses, then mix in the cocoa, dates, and flour. Grease a 7½-inch diameter ovenproof ceramic bowl (about a 1½-quart capacity).

Pour the batter into the ceramic bowl. Coat a piece of waxed paper with cooking spray and place over the bowl, pressing down on top of the pudding. Cover the ceramic bowl tightly with aluminum foil and secure with kitchen twine for a tight seal.

Place a small rack at the bottom of an 8-quart stock pot, and carefully lower down the covered bowl. The rack should just keep the bowl from touching the bottom of the pot. Fill the stock pot with water reaching halfway up, about 4 inches. Set the stock pot over medium heat and bring to a boil, then cover the stockpot and steam the pudding for 1 hour, checking the water level and adding more as necessary. A toothpick inserted into the pudding will come out clean when done. If the pudding is not ready after 1 hour, continue to cook, checking every 10 minutes.

When the pudding is done, remove it from the stockpot wearing large oven mitts to protect your arms from the steam. Loosen the edges of the foil around the bowl, and cool the pudding on a wire rack.

Just before serving, make the hard sauce: Heat the unsalted butter, cream, vanilla, and the remaining cup of sugar in a small sauté pan over medium heat. Cook, stirring constantly, until heated through and smooth. Remove from the pan, drizzle over the pudding, and serve immediately.

BEVERAGE PAIRINGS

An Austrian Pinot Blanc will cut through the creaminess of the cheese log and highlight its earthy qualities to good effect. The beer pairing has to be a Kölsch: its gentle hops play well with the cheese, while its malty and crisp character perfectly accents the toasty pine nuts.

For the crudités shot, a Falanghina from the Italian region of Sannio provides complementary flavors of fresh melon and almond. An American wheat beer will also highlight its fresh vegetable flavors extremely well.

The stuffed mushrooms need a pairing with full body and intense spiciness. A Grenache Blanc from the Central Coast of California fits the bill. A Scotch ale also works, plus it offers a smokiness that accents the mushrooms to maximum effect.

For the beef stew, you are going to want a mind-blowing pairing, something that offers up the secrets of animal and earth in a single glass. That would be a Cornas from the Northern Rhône region of France. There really isn't a beer equivalent to that wine. However, feel free to pair the beer used to braise the dish, a Belgian tripel, for a nice complement when serving.

The steamed pudding is a whiplash of flavors and deserves an equally compelling wine pairing. Pedro Ximénez, a dessert Sherry from Spain with caramel, almond, and cream notes, wields a backbone of bitter orange that keeps it from becoming cloying, and is my top pick.

SPRING

SUNSHINE! It's like the world became an old school Disney film overnight: The birds are singing, the house mice are chatting away, foxes are rakishly twirling their tails. YOU HALF EXPECT A HAPPY LITTLE CANARY TO FLUTTER ONTO YOUR SHOULDER AS YOU WALK OUTSIDE. The first spring day is so breathtaking it seems like a fantasy; after months of winter this perfect feeling can be more startling than a bunch of anthropomorphized animals skipping through your neighborhood.

Everywhere you look, nature is turning from brown to bright green. The change is most stark in gardens and farmlands, where the first buds are poking out of the cool earth. As the season progresses, things keep changing. YOUR COLOR-STARVED EYES BECOME ENCHANTED BY ASPARAGUS, THEN BEETS, THEN GARLIC SCAPES, THEN FAVA BEANS, AND ON AND ON THROUGHOUT THE SEASON. It's easy to believe that you never really understood what "fresh" meant until this very moment.

To capture the unadulterated excitement of this season, each spring chapter centers around the ever-changing bounty of our local farms. I SUGGEST DOING MOST OF YOUR GROCERY SHOPPING AT YOUR LOCAL FARMERS' MARKET AT THIS TIME OF THE YEAR, and not just because of the amazing produce and the many ways buying local benefits the community. Strolling through the market on a Sunday morning and enjoying this bounty is nothing short of pure romance: selecting eggs and flowers from a young Amish farmer, tasting an assortment of aged cheddars by a local cheese maker, noshing on a buttery and crisp croissant from the neighborhood baker. Truthfully, THE GREATEST LOVE AFFAIR OF MY LIFE BEGAN WITH FINDING THE PERFECT ASPARAGUS SPEARS with my date at one of Philadelphia's famous farmers' markets. Those stalks later turned into Asparagus Chowder (page 154), and the relationship became the real thing.

EARLY SPRING DINNER

In the early spring only a handful of vegetables are coming into season. The asparagus will be svelte and delicate, the beets will be extra-sweet, and the greens will be shockingly peppery. Let's make the most of them!

Since it's still cool outside, it's important to play with some richer flavors and textures in our dishes. The following recipes act as a bridge between the comfort food of winter and the fresher tastes of spring.

For a specific type of lushness and weight in this dinner, I use crème fraîche. This is a decadently rich ingredient exhibiting a lightly grassy and citrus-accented flavor. If you've never heard of it, that's not surprising: A staple in Continental cooking, crème fraîche is nearly unknown here in the States. Because it is such a versatile ingredient, I always keep a small amount on hand. After preparing these dishes it's likely that you will, too.

This is an ideal menu for two to four people, although I once prepared it during a cooking class for twenty people with great success. It's one of the easiest and most refreshing menus in this book.

Chilled Asparagus with Pepperoncini-Orange Vinaigrette

It's all about the asparagus in this recipe; selecting the perfect spears will be critical. Look for the thinnest stalks and make sure the tips are free of any rotten bits. Don't worry if the bottoms of the stalks are dry or bleached looking; you will be removing them before serving.

SERVES 4 TO 6

¼ CUP PLUS ¾ TEASPOON FINE SALT, DIVIDED

2 CUPS ICE (CRUSHED OR CUBED)

2 CUPS COLD WATER

1 BUNCH ASPARAGUS (ABOUT 12 TO 14 STALKS),
    WHITE ENDS TRIMMED AND DISCARDED

5 PEPPERONCINI (SWEET ITALIAN PEPPERS), DICED

1 TABLESPOON ORANGE JUICE

2 TABLESPOONS EXTRA-VIRGIN OLIVE OIL

In a large pot over high heat, bring 2 quarts of water mixed with ¼ cup of the salt to a rolling boil.

Prepare an ice bath in a large mixing bowl with the ice and 2 cups of cold water.

Cook the asparagus in the boiling water for 1 minute, or just until the spears turn bright green. Drain the asparagus, and plunge the spears into the ice bath. Let the asparagus chill for 5 minutes, or until the stalks feel ice-cold to the touch. Remove the asparagus and pat dry. Reserve.

Combine the pepperoncini, orange juice, olive oil, and the remaining ¾ teaspoon of salt to a small mixing bowl and whisk until well combined. Drizzle over the reserved asparagus and serve immediately.

Roasted Beet Salad with Arugula and Goat Cheese

I forgot how much I love beets until I re-created this classic recipe. Goat cheese and roasted beets are simply a great combination and the crème fraîche acts as a minister: it perfectly marries the flavors. When peeling the beets, be prepared to have your hands dyed bright red. You may even want to don latex gloves for this step, but don't worry: the stain will come off with a bit of soap and water.

SERVES 4

3 SMALL BEETS, LEAVES AND ENDS TRIMMED AND DISCARDED

1 SMALL BUNCH ARUGULA (ABOUT 1 CUP), TORN INTO BITE-SIZE PIECES

2 TABLESPOONS CHOPPED WALNUTS

2 TABLESPOONS CRÈME FRAÎCHE (PAGE 142)

1 TEASPOON FINE SALT

½ TEASPOON FRESHLY GROUND BLACK PEPPER

4 OUNCES GOAT CHEESE

Preheat the oven to 375°F. Wrap the trimmed beets in aluminum foil and roast them for about 1 hour, or until they can be easily pierced with a paring knife.

Remove the beets from the oven, and let them rest for 30 minutes, or until they are cool enough to handle. Peel the beets using a sharp paring knife, and slice them into ½-inch cubes. Set aside.

To assemble the salad: Place the beets, arugula, walnuts, crème fraîche, salt, and pepper in a large mixing bowl and toss well to combine. Garnish each serving with small chunks of the goat cheese, and serve immediately.

Crème Fraîche

Crème fraîche is basically a simple homemade cheese made with heavy cream. It must be maintained at room temperature for the first three days as it transforms from cream to crème. Afterward, it can be kept in an airtight container in the refrigerator for up to ten days.

MAKES 3 CUPS

3 CUPS HEAVY CREAM

¼ CUP BUTTERMILK

In a large bowl, mix the heavy cream and the buttermilk. Lightly cover the bowl with a clean kitchen towel, and let it stand at room temperature for 48 hours, or until the mixture thickens to the consistency of cake frosting. Transfer the crème fraîche to an airtight container and store in the refrigerator for up to 10 days.

Caramelized Scallops with English Pickles and Crème Fraîche

The tender taste and texture of scallops can serve as a red meat substitute, depending on their level of freshness. The best scallops will not have even a hint of fishiness about them. For scallops with fewer additives, seek out the more expensive "dry packed" kind—these contain zero preservatives. Pickled cucumbers are added here to counter the richness of the scallops while also complementing their sweetness.

SERVES 4 TO 6

2 CUPS WHITE VINEGAR

2 TEASPOONS CURRY POWDER

½ CUP GRANULATED SUGAR

2 LARGE CUCUMBERS, SLICED INTO 1-INCH-ROUNDS

1 POUND SEA SCALLOPS

3 TABLESPOONS EXTRA-VIRGIN OLIVE OIL

1½ TEASPOONS FINE SALT

1 TEASPOON FRESHLY GROUND BLACK PEPPER

½ CUP CRÈME FRAÎCHE (PAGE 142)

In a large mixing bowl, whisk together the vinegar, curry powder, and sugar. Add the cucumbers, cover the bowl with plastic wrap, and transfer it to the refrigerator. Let the mixture stand for at least 4 hours, or overnight.

In another large mixing bowl, toss the scallops with the oil, salt, and pepper. Heat a sauté pan over high heat and when it's very hot, add the scallops, being careful not to crowd the pan. Cook, undisturbed, until golden-brown, about 2 minutes for small scallops or 4 minutes for larger ones. Flip the scallops and sear for another 2 to 4 minutes.

Divide the crème fraîche, the scallops, and the pickles equally among each serving plate. For a dramatic presentation, place a pickle on each plate and top with a dollop of crème fraîche, then a scallop. Serve immediately.

Chocolate Pot de Crème Fraîche with Dark Cherries

This is so easy to make it's reckless. A suggestion regarding cherries: perfectly ripe ones will be firm and still have their stems attached. Also, when melting the chocolate, take care to not overheat the mixture; a rapid boil will curdle the mixture and ruin the dish.

SERVES 4

2¼ CUPS CRÈME FRAÎCHE

12 OUNCES DARK CHOCOLATE, CHOPPED INTO SMALL PIECES

DARK CHERRIES, HALVED WITH PITS REMOVED, FOR GARNISH

Place the crème fraîche in a medium saucepan over medium heat. Stir the crème fraîche until it comes to a simmer, reduce heat to low, and then add the chopped chocolate. Stir the mixture until the chocolate melts and it becomes smooth, about 5 minutes. Remove from heat.

Pour the mixture into four 2-ounce soufflé cups arranged on a rimmed baking sheet and cover tightly. Transfer the baking sheet to the refrigerator and chill for at least 2 hours or until firm. Serve with a garnish of cherries.

BEVERAGE PAIRINGS

Asparagus is a quandary: it's a wonderful accompaniment to other food, but very hard to pair with beverages. While its lovely grassy and herbal accents are a great counterpoint to many dishes, these same notes add a metallic taste to most wines and beers. There really are only two pairings that consistently work well on the beverage front: Sancerre and wit beer. Sancerre is a Sauvignon Blanc grown around the town of Sancerre in France, and a wit beer is a Belgian ale made with wheat. Both possess a pleasing grassiness that works as an effective flavor camouflage for the asparagus.

Yet another Sauvignon Blanc pairs well with the beet salad, this one from the Casablanca Valley in Chile. The steely edge of the wine cuts through the tanginess of the cheese and brings out the roasted nuance of the beets. Of course, you could also just keep on drinking the Sancerre; it's a very good match as well.

For the scallops, I must suggest a Sauvignon Blanc again. This is really a one-grape kind of dinner. The sweetness of the scallops and the pickles play effortlessly off of the grapefruit flavors in the wine. Either of the two Sauvignon Blancs recommended above will work. For a mind-blowing beer pairing, pick up a Flanders brown, if you can. It is a uniquely aged Belgian ale that walks a fine balance of sweet and sour. It will synchronize perfectly with the brightness of this dish.

I am not a fan of pairing the pot de crème with alcoholic beverages, as the combination can sour the belly. The best pairing is actually coffee. The perfect cup is a full city (aka Viennese) roast of Ethiopian Yirgacheffe. It has a unique balance of chocolate and floral notes that are supremely elegant, and adds a pleasing contrast of temperatures on the palate.

RAINY DAY NOSH

When I started writing this chapter it had been overcast for three days straight. This is what I wrote: "The cold rainy days in early spring are depressing. The rain is so cold that it feels like winter snuck back into your bones. You look out the window and the neighborhood is a globe of puffy gray, like the sails of a ghost ship."

I continued on like that for another six hundred words, like a modern day Nietzsche engaging in Def Jam poetry. But even the happiest person can fall prey to the blues during a rainy spell in the first weeks of springtime.

Cooking up some comfort food is one great way to break up that funk. Keeping a kitchen full of easy-to-use ingredients is essential for doing combat with depressing weather. So before you get caught like I did, head to the market and stock up on these essential staples—along with the requisite onions, garlic, and olive oil—to fill your pantry.

The first on our battle list has to be stone-ground grits: with a little maple syrup, it's great for breakfast; with a bit of cheddar cheese, it's an addictive side dish; with head-on shrimp and andouille sausage, it's revelatory.

Don't skimp on the starch. You should have some fresh pasta sheets in the freezer, too. The Wild Boar(ish) Ragu with Pappardelle (page 150) recipe will blow your mind. But even a dish as simple as browned butter with shallots will taste phenomenal if you use fresh pasta.

You should always have a few really good cheeses on hand as well. Hard cheeses, like aged cheddar and Parmesan, are great for both cooking and snacking. Soft cheeses, like ricotta and chèvre, will allow you to create all types of dishes, from salad to dessert.

Make sure to buy asparagus, zucchini, and spinach. Their uses are endless because they can be added to almost any type of meal. In a similar vein, always keep fresh herbs on hand; with a bunch each of sage and basil, you can flavor almost any dish like a professional.

Proteins like sausage and prosciutto are great to keep in stock, too. They can serve as either the star of your comfort meal or as part of an ensemble cast. Shrimp are versatile enough to make our list because they can go from frozen to fully cooked in about ten minutes.

Enjoy your rainy day nosh, and if you still feel like you want to sit in a dark corner and write existential prose, then maybe it's time to funnel your creativity into the kitchen. The world needs more tasty recipes; you can trust me (and my editor) that what it doesn't need is more bad poetry.

Shrimp and Grits

This is a classic low-country preparation. Finding head-on shrimp can be difficult, but it lends the dish a deep, authentic flavor. If you can't find them—or those buggy eyes simply freak you out—use headless, medium-large shrimp instead.

SERVES 4 TO 6

1 CUP REGULAR CHICKEN STOCK

¾ TEASPOON FINE SALT

1 CUP STONE-GROUND GRITS

2 TABLESPOONS UNSALTED BUTTER

2 TABLESPOONS VEGETABLE OIL

6 GARLIC CLOVES, MINCED

½ TEASPOON WHITE PEPPER

1 TEASPOON RED PEPPER FLAKES

¼ CUP ANDOUILLE SAUSAGE, DICED

1 SMALL SPANISH ONION (ABOUT ½ CUP), DICED

1 POUND HEAD-ON SHRIMP, PEELED AND DEVEINED

½ CUP DRY WHITE WINE

Add the chicken stock, salt, and 3 cups of water to a large saucepan set over medium-high heat and bring to a boil. Slowly add the grits, whisking constantly to make sure the grains do not clump together. Reduce the heat to medium and simmer for 15 minutes, stirring about every 3 minutes. The grits should be thick when done.

While the grits are simmering, make the shrimp. Add the butter and oil to a large sauté pan over medium heat. At the moment the butter starts to bubble, add the garlic, white pepper, red pepper flakes, and sausage. Sauté for 1 more minute or until the garlic starts to turn golden-brown. Add the onions and sauté for another minute, until they start to turn translucent. Push the onions and sausage to the edge of the pan and add the shrimp in a single layer. Turn up to medium-high heat and cook undisturbed for 1 minute, or until the shrimp starts to turn pink. Flip over the shrimp and sauté for another 30 seconds or until the shrimp has turned completely pink.

Add the white wine to the sauté pan and bring the mixture to a boil. Cook until the wine has reduced by half, about 2 minutes. Serve immediately over a heaping spoonful of grits.

Wild Boar(ish) Ragu with Pappardelle

Over the past few years wild boar ragu has become a trendy dish. But for the home cook it's nearly impossible to find the key ingredient. I don't know anyone outside of the restaurant industry—aside from Michael Pollan—who can source wild boar in the U.S. Pork sausage, with the same deeply nuanced and intense pork flavors, serves as the ideal substitute. No one but your Italian nonna will be able to tell the difference.

SERVES 4 TO 6

2 TABLESPOONS EXTRA-VIRGIN OLIVE OIL

1 POUND SWEET ITALIAN SAUSAGE, CASINGS REMOVED

2 ANCHOVY FILLETS PACKED IN OIL

5 GARLIC CLOVES, SMASHED

2 SMALL YELLOW ONIONS (ABOUT 2 CUPS), ROUGHLY CHOPPED

1½ TEASPOONS RED PEPPER FLAKES

1 TEASPOON SMOKED PAPRIKA

2 CARROTS (ABOUT ½ CUP), PEELED AND CHOPPED

1 TABLESPOON FINE SALT, PLUS MORE AS NEEDED

2 CUPS RED WINE, PREFERABLY A CHIANTI

1 CUP BEEF STOCK

1 (26-OUNCE) JAR GOOD-QUALITY MARINARA SAUCE

1 POUND DRIED PAPPARDELLE OR 2 SHEETS OF FRESH PASTA (PAGE 173), ROLLED OUT PAPER THIN

Preheat a large, heavy bottomed pot over medium-high heat for 5 minutes, then add the olive oil. Once the oil just begins to smoke (just a little!) add the sausage, anchovies, garlic, onion, and red pepper flakes. Cook, stirring occasionally and crumbling the sausage with your spatula, until the onions turn brown and the sausage is cooked, about 10 minutes. Add the paprika and carrots and cook for 10 more minutes, until the carrots have softened and begun to brown.

Add the salt, wine, and beef stock, increase the heat to high, and bring to a boil. Reduce to a simmer and cook, uncovered, for about 20 minutes, or until the mixture has thickened slightly.

Add the tomato sauce, return the mixture to a boil, and reduce the heat enough to maintain a gentle simmer. Simmer the sauce, uncovered, for another 30 minutes, or until the sausage begins to dissolve into the sauce.

Remove the sauce from the heat and let it cool to room temperature, about 2 hours.

When the sauce has cooled, ladle the mixture into a food processor, and zap it twice for 10 seconds each time. The resulting sauce should be chunky.

Place the sauce in a large pot set over medium heat and cover. Reheat the sauce while you cook the dried pappardelle according to the package's directions, or while you prepare the fresh pasta.

For fresh pappardelle: Cut the pasta sheets into 1-inch-thick ribbons. Don't worry about being perfect, as this dish looks best when the pasta is a bit uneven in width.

Cooking the pasta, however, has to be precise and quick. Place a large pot of water over high heat. Add fine salt until the water tastes briny, like the ocean (usually about 2 to 3 tablespoons). Once the water comes to a rolling boil, drop pasta by the handful into the water in small batches. Remove carefully with tongs the moment it rises to the top, and shake gently to remove any excess water. Immediately add the pasta to the sauce.

Toss the pasta with the sauce using a soft touch, then serve immediately.

Fresh Ricotta Gnocchi with Sage Butter

Gnocchi is usually reserved as a restaurant treat. Even I was afraid of trying it in my home until I experimented with the following recipe. This preparation yields light-as-a-cloud gnocchi that couldn't be easier to make. Note the absence of salt in the dough; this ensures that the small pillows will not fall apart when cooked.

SERVES 4 TO 6

Ricotta Gnocchi
1 (16-OUNCE) CONTAINER WHOLE MILK RICOTTA
1 LARGE EGG
½ CUP FINELY GRATED PARMESAN (OR PECORINO CHEESE)
¾ CUP ALL-PURPOSE FLOUR, PLUS ½ CUP MORE FOR DUSTING

Sage Butter
4 TABLESPOONS (1 STICK) UNSALTED BUTTER
1 SHALLOT, DICED
1 TEASPOON KOSHER SALT
¼ TEASPOON FRESHLY GROUND BLACK PEPPER
6 FRESH SAGE LEAVES, TORN INTO STRIPS

Place the ricotta in a cheese-cloth lined strainer over a larger mixing bowl and store, uncovered, in the refrigerator overnight to drain excess water from the ricotta. In the morning, discard the accumulated liquid in the bottom of the bowl.

To make the gnocchi: Mix the strained ricotta, egg, cheese, and ¾ cup of the flour together in a large bowl until all of the ingredients are thoroughly incorporated. Cover and refrigerate for 30 minutes.

After this resting period, the dough should feel slightly sticky, like masking tape. If it feels more like raw cookie dough, then add more flour, about 1 tablespoon at a time, until it reaches the right consistency. If you added more than 2 tablespoons of extra flour, cover and refrigerate for an additional 15 minutes before continuing.

Form the dough into two balls, return it to the bowl, cover, and refrigerate for another 30 minutes. Sprinkle your hands and the work surface with a light dusting of flour. Roll one of the dough balls into a ½-inch-thick log about 18 inches long. To form the gnocchi, cut the log into ¾-inch pieces. Lay the finished gnocchi in a single layer on a sheet tray lightly dusted with flour. Repeat with the next ball of dough.

Place a large salted pot of water over high heat and bring to a boil.

To make the sage butter: While you are waiting for the water to boil, add the butter to a large sauté pan over medium heat. Add the shallot, salt, and pepper, and cook until both the butter and shallot turn golden-brown, about 3 minutes. Remove from heat, add the sage, cover to keep warm, and reserve.

When the water has come to a boil, carefully drop in a handful of gnocchi, and as soon as the pasta floats to the top, about 2 minutes, scoop it up with a slotted spoon and transfer to a large serving bowl. Cover to keep warm. Cook the gnocchi in batches this way until all pasta is cooked.

Drizzle the gnocchi with the sage butter and toss to combine. Serve immediately.

Asparagus Chowder

I may get my "New Englander for life" status revoked with this recipe. Honestly, you don't need clams to make a great chowder. This is a wonderful vegetarian option for a rainy day, and it shows what magic you can whip up with a few humble ingredients.

SERVES 4 TO 6

1 TABLESPOON EXTRA-VIRGIN OLIVE OIL

1 LARGE SPANISH ONION, DICED (ABOUT 1½ CUPS)

1 TEASPOON DRIED THYME

1 TEASPOON DRIED MARJORAM

½ CUP WHITE WINE

¾ POUND NEW POTATOES, CUT INTO 1-INCH CUBES

1 LARGE CARROT, PEELED AND CUT INTO 1-INCH CUBES

1 CELERY STALK, CUT INTO 1-INCH CUBES

2 POUNDS ASPARAGUS, ENDS TRIMMED AND SPEARS CUT IN HALF

½ CUP HEAVY CREAM

2 TEASPOONS FINE SALT

1 TEASPOON WHITE PEPPER

Add the olive oil to a large pot over medium-high heat, and sauté the onion, thyme, and marjoram until the onion turns translucent, about 3 minutes. Add 3½ cups water, the white wine, potatoes, carrot, and celery. Bring the mixture to a boil, cover, and reduce the heat to a simmer. Cook until the potatoes are soft, about 15 minutes. Add the asparagus and continue simmering for 5 minutes, or until the asparagus has turned bright green.

Let the soup cool for 30 minutes, then ladle it into a food processor, along with the cream, salt, and pepper. Purée until smooth. (An immersion blender may also be used for this step.) Taste and season if necessary, then serve immediately.

BEVERAGE PAIRINGS

On a rainy day, my first suggestion is to not go outside at all and drink whatever you have in the cabinet. If you are willing to brave the weather, then I have a few suggestions. For the Shrimp and Grits, the best wine pairing is a Fumé Blanc from California. This is a Sauvignon Blanc that has been oak-aged. For beer, I want to have an India pale ale. Both selections will bring out the earthy sweetness of the shrimp while not interfering with the spicy top notes in the dish.

For the Wild Boar(ish) Ragu, I say go big: there is nothing refined or elegant about this meal, so your wine should have a similar personality. A Petite Sirah from the North Coast of California is the best bet here. If you do it right, you will be covered in red wine and tomato sauce by the end of this meal.

The Ricotta Gnocchi is a special dish, having a lightness of texture draped in toasted shallot and herb flavors. The right wine for this is a Syrah from Santa Ynez in California; it has a similar texture to the dish. For beer, seek out a Kölsch. If you are really daring, there are some great Kölsch-style beers from Northern Italy with the perfect balance of hoppiness and acidity for this creamy entrée.

Finally, for the Asparagus Chowder: As mentioned in the Early Spring Dinner chapter (page 139), this vegetable is quite difficult to pair with wine. Two different beer and wine cocktails work very well, however, owing to the creaminess of the soup. A shandygaff is one-part pale ale and one-part ginger ale, served in a pint glass. The other is the black velvet, which is half porter and half sparkling wine, served in a champagne flute.

SPRINGTIME BRUNCH PARTY

T he social season begins anew each spring, making this the perfect opportunity to host an easy brunch. The simple mantra behind this menu is kind to guest and host alike: to every extent possible allow your guests to create their own dishes and drinks from a creative array of ingredients.

To accomplish this task, however, it is key to lay out every detail of the party beforehand. I freely admit that I am an odd duck: I forget to pay my mortgage, but I plan out my parties as if I were General Petraeus on his last mission. Sure, it's not like you will save the free world, but you will find that good party planning will keep the peace in your own home.

First, refer to the introduction of the Wintertime House Party (page 121 for guidance on setting up space in your home appropriately. If more than a dozen folks will be attending your brunch, separate the food and beverage stations by placing one indoors and the other outdoors. (Preferably the food should stay indoors to ensure it stays at room temperature.) Another suggestion: using hand-written tags to identify dishes or ingredients will save you from having to reel off the details to every guest. The recipes below assume a guest count of between ten to fifteen people.

The Bloody Bar

A Bloody Mary is a perfectly acceptable first course at any brunch. I like to think of it as gazpacho accented with vodka. Your guests can mix and match spicy and savory notes to their hearts' content with the ingredients recommended here. Place a one-ounce shot glass on the bar to help everyone measure their vodka pours before mixing. Also, use a large ice bucket to keep the various components cold, such as a 20-gallon galvanized steel tub. Long plastic spoons can serve as disposable stirrers; chopsticks also work well and add a fun touch.

TOMATO JUICE. The foundation of the Bloody. Allow for at least 16 ounces per person, enough for two drinks. Serve in large pitchers.

CLAM JUICE. A classic New England addition. A squirt will inject a touch of brininess and will make the drink taste like the ocean. It's also great with beer and a splash of tomato juice. Decant the clam juice in a squeeze bottle.

HORSERADISH. The classic; no Bloody is complete without it. A jar of prepared grated horseradish will be easiest to serve (although purchasing fresh horseradish and placing it on the buffet with a micrograter is an option as well). You won't need more than 4 ounces for two dozen people. Serve in a small bowl with a spoon.

BLACK PEPPER. A large grinder works best in this setting, both for the fresh burst of flavor and the fun factor it provides.

CELERY STALKS. Make sure these aren't browning and are washed well to remove sand. Keep the leaves on for presentation, and serve on a platter or in a pitcher.

HOT SAUCE. The spicier the better, but keep it red (none of that fancy green stuff). One small bottle is plenty.

VODKA. Make sure it's ice-cold and unflavored. One (750 ml) bottle for every fifteen guests is advisable.

KOSHER SALT. Serve 4 to 6 tablespoons in a bowl with a small spoon.

CUCUMBER. Slice into quarter-inch-thick rounds. A great chef's trick: before cutting, run a fork down the sides to break up the skin; this will make them easier to eat. One cucumber is enough for up to twenty people. Serve in a bowl with tongs.

WHOLE PEPPERONCINI. This is a great (and often neglected) garnish; it adds a piercing splash of vinegar and spice. One cup of these puppies for every ten guests is enough. Serve in a bowl with tongs.

LEMONS. Slice into paper-thin rounds. This is another great garnish that adds a lively freshness to the drink. One lemon for every twenty guests works well. Serve in a bowl with tongs.

The Modern Classic

The following ingredients make a well-rounded drink on their own, and also serve as the base for my own variations, The New Englander and The European Girlfriend.

SERVES 1

1 TEASPOON PREPARED HORSERADISH

2 DASHES RED PEPPER SAUCE

1 TEASPOON KOSHER SALT

½ TEASPOON FRESHLY GROUND BLACK PEPPER

2 OUNCES VODKA

¼ CUP ICE CUBES

12 OUNCES TOMATO JUICE

2 LEMON ROUNDS, FOR GARNISH

1 CUCUMBER ROUND, FOR GARNISH

In a pint glass, combine the horseradish, red pepper sauce, salt, black pepper, and vodka. Add the ice and tomato juice. Shake well and garnish with lemon and cucumber. Serve.

The New Englander

To create this variation, use The Modern Classic ingredients but reduce the amount of tomato juice to 11 ounces, omit the salt, and add 1 ounce of clam juice.

The European Girlfriend

For this variation, combine 11 ounces of tomato juice, 3 ounces of vodka, and add a pepperoncini garnish.

The Egg Bar

A few years ago in Portland, Oregon, I had an egg sandwich that blew my mind. The balance of grease and bread and flavor was such that I am pretty sure I had a glimpse of Nirvana. This egg bar pays homage to that perfect breakfast sandwich.

FRESH SMALL ROLLS, SLICED. Obtain freshly baked, if possible. If not, purchase frozen parbaked rolls and bake them according to the package instructions. Serve sliced in half on a large cutting board.

SMOKED SALMON. Yes, this is costly. Figure on 1 ounce per person. Some supermarkets sell smoked salmon scraps, which are just as good and cost much less. Arrange in a single layer on a large plate to serve.

SMOKED TROUT. Serve 1 ounce per person. Smoked trout can be a more interesting addition to a breakfast sandwich than salmon. Make sure to remove the skin before placing on a serving platter.

SOUR CREAM. One 14-ounce carton is more than enough, unless you are planning on hosting a busload of Norwegians.

SHALLOT, DICED. You are going to need a lot; dice one large shallot per every ten people.

ROASTED RED PEPPERS. Cut into 2-inch-thick ribbons. It's cheaper to buy this ingredient in jars from the grocery, so don't bother roasting them at home. A 16-ounce jar per twenty people is enough.

ANCHOVIES. One 2-ounce, oil-packed tin will serve twenty people. Do not dare neglect this ingredient; it's the key to my amazing breakfast sandwich.

SHARP CHEDDAR CHEESE. Sliced thin, about 8 ounces per every twenty people.

BABY SPINACH. Serve only fresh, whole leaves. One pound per twenty people is more than enough.

KETCHUP. You gotta have a bottle; this is America. Try to find the homemade variety at your local farmers' market or gourmet grocery store. Better yet, make your own Homemade Ketchup (page 20).

THICK-CUT BACON. Two pounds per twenty people. To cook, roast in the oven at 350°F on a rimmed baking sheet, about 20 minutes, until the bacon is crisp.

EGGS, SCRAMBLED. You will need three dozen eggs per every twenty people. See The Perfect Scrambled Eggs (page 87). Plan on cooking a batch every 15 minutes so they remain fresh and warm.

BAGELS. Provide a half dozen per every ten folks.

The Walter Cronkite

SERVES 1

1 ROLL

2 EGGS, SCRAMBLED

1 SLICE CHEDDAR CHEESE

1 TABLESPOON KETCHUP

1 SLICE ROASTED RED PEPPER

2 ANCHOVIES

1 SLICE BACON

Slice the roll in half, and layer the eggs and cheese. Add the ketchup, and continue layering the sandwich with the red pepper, anchovy, and bacon. Place the top of the roll back on, and serve.

The Scandy Bastard

SERVES 1

1 BAGEL, TOASTED

1 OUNCE SMOKED SALMON

1 OUNCE SMOKED TROUT

2 TABLESPOONS SOUR CREAM

2 TEASPOONS SHALLOTS

¼ CUP FRESH SPINACH

On a toasted bagel half, layer the salmon and trout. Spread the sour cream over the fish, and sprinkle the shallots evenly. Finish with spinach. Place the top half of the bagel on the sandwich and serve.

The Good Ole Coco Brown

SERVES 1

1 ROLL

2 SLICES BACON

1 SLICE CHEDDAR CHEESE

2 EGGS, SCRAMBLED

1 TEASPOON KETCHUP

The classic. On the roll, layer the bacon, the cheddar, and the eggs. Finish with the squirt of ketchup.

Banana Bread

This recipe yields a moist bread with a lovely, crisp crust. It is essential to not overmix the dough; a dough that becomes too smooth will make for a rubbery bread.

MAKES 1 LOAF

1¾ CUPS ALL-PURPOSE FLOUR

¾ CUP GRANULATED SUGAR

1 TEASPOON BAKING POWDER

¼ TEASPOON BAKING SODA

¼ TEASPOON FINE SALT

1 TEASPOON GROUND CINNAMON

1 CUP WALNUTS, CHOPPED

3 BANANAS (ABOUT 1 POUND)

2 LARGE EGGS, LIGHTLY BEATEN

2 STICKS (½ CUP) UNSALTED BUTTER, AT ROOM TEMPERATURE

1 TEASPOON PURE VANILLA EXTRACT

CREAM CHEESE, FOR SERVING

FRUIT JAMS (STRAWBERRY, LEMON CURD, ORANGE MARMALADE, AND LINGONBERRY), FOR SERVING

Preheat oven to 350°F. Grease a 9 x 5 x 3-inch loaf pan with cooking spray.

In a large bowl, combine the flour, sugar, baking powder, baking soda, salt, cinnamon, and nuts. Set aside.

In a medium-sized bowl, mash together the bananas, eggs, butter, and vanilla. The mixture should have the consistency of pudding. With a wooden spoon, gently fold this banana mixture into the flour mixture. The resulting batter should be thick and chunky.

Scrape the batter into the prepared pan. Bake for 1 hour, or until the bread turns golden-brown. To check whether the bread is done, insert a toothpick into the center of the loaf. If it comes out clean, the bread is ready. Place the pan on a wire rack to cool, and then remove the bread from the pan. Slice in half lengthwise, then cut into ½-inch-thick slices. Serve warm or at room temperature with cream cheese and jam.

THE SPARKLY SPRITZER BAR

No brunch is complete without some bubbly. For goodness sakes, don't splurge on real Champagne: it's way too classy for our purposes. We want bubbles that are a bit more forgiving and fun-loving. My top four picks are: a Crémant de Vouvray from France, a Cava from Spain, a Prosecco from Italy, and a sparkling wine from the Sonoma Valley. You should provide at least one bottle for every ten guests.

I love flirty cocktails, but my very nature abhors adulterating wines with juices and stuff. It's silly, but I can't watch someone drinking a white wine spritzer. When it comes to brunch, however, I am an unabashed hypocrite. On Sunday afternoons only, I love adding all sorts of fun flavors to my bubbly. I've even gone so far as to create a few special ones myself.

There are three elixirs I don't go without: orange juice, mango purée, and rhubarb syrup.

Mango Purée

MAKES 8 OUNCES

4 MANGOES, PEELED AND PITTED

¼ CUP ORANGE JUICE, FRESH OR BOTTLED

Cut the mangoes into chunks and purée in a food processor. Strain through a fine-mesh sieve, discarding the pulp. Stir the mango juice together with the orange juice. Transfer to a small pitcher or a squirt bottle, and chill before serving.

Rhubarb Syrup

MAKES 8 OUNCES

1 POUND RHUBARB, ROUGHLY CHOPPED

¼ CUP GRANULATED SUGAR

Combine the rhubarb, sugar, and 2 cups of water in a saucepan set over high heat. Bring the mixture to a boil for 10 minutes without stirring, until the rhubarb starts to collapse and the sugar melts. Strain the mixture through a fine mesh sieve, pressing on the rhubarb to release all the juices, and transfer it to a small pitcher or a squirt bottle. Cover, if necessary, and chill in the refrigerator for 2 hours before serving.

SPRINGTIME BRUNCH PARTY

The San Sebastian

SERVES 1

1 TABLESPOON MANGO PURÉE

6 OUNCES SPARKLING WINE

Drizzle the purée into a champagne flute. Slowly add the wine, and serve.

The Morning Proposal

SERVES 1

2 TABLESPOONS RHUBARB SYRUP

1 TABLESPOON ORANGE JUICE

4 OUNCES SPARKLING WINE

Pour syrup into the bottom of a champagne flute. Slowly add the wine.
Finish with the orange juice. Serve.

Rosie's Secret

SERVES 1

1 TABLESPOON ORANGE JUICE

1 TABLESPOON MANGO PURÉE

1 OUNCE VODKA

5 OUNCES SPARKLING WINE

In a champagne flute, add the orange juice, the mango, and the vodka.
Finish with the sparkling wine and serve.

ELEGANT DINNER

I am a twenty-first century guy. You know the type: too jocular, too earnest, too wired, too ironic, and way too anxious. A man like me would never be mistaken for an aristocrat. Perversely, that fact inspired me to spend weeks creating a singularly elegant dinner.

In this chapter, I take inspiration from the middle of the last century, when men were men . . . who ate Jello. It was a time when, notwithstanding the fruit in a mold, cuisine was much more formal than it is today. The top restaurants were luxurious damask-and-chandelier affairs and menus featured beef Wellington, lobster Thermidor, and crêpes Suzette. It was an era of American style seen through the haze of a continental past.

That cuisine is generally too heavy for a springtime meal—beef Wellington is pretty much coronary disease on a plate—but I wanted to use its aesthetic as a jumping off point for creating an elegant home cooked meal. My method was to fuse elements of that time with another era that saw a resurgence in elegant dining—the late twentieth century. While the flavors and presentations here are quite modern, the recipes include whimsical mid-century touches that pay homage to the high style of the past.

Belgian Endive with Walnuts and Blue Cheese

This salad oozes "natty nineties" but still looks beautiful plated up. When preparing the endive, make sure to remove the outer leaves, any brown-stained leaves, and the hard core, or the salad will be too bitter. Also, stay away from any cheese labeled "Gorgonzola piccante" because it will be too intense for this dish.

SERVES 4 TO 6

1 TEASPOON FRESHLY SQUEEZED LEMON JUICE

1 TEASPOON DIJON MUSTARD

2 TABLESPOONS EXTRA-VIRGIN OLIVE OIL

1 BELGIAN ENDIVE HEAD, QUARTERED LENGTHWISE

2 TABLESPOONS CRUMBLED GORGONZOLA

2 TABLESPOONS CRUSHED WALNUTS

To make the vinaigrette: Combine the lemon juice, mustard, and olive oil in a large mixing bowl, and whisk until well combined. Add the endive and toss to coat thoroughly with the dressing. Garnish each plate with a sprinkle of cheese and walnuts. Serve immediately.

Homemade Pea and Almond Ravioli in Brown Butter Sauce

This is not a simple recipe, but it's the easiest ravioli recipe you will ever find. The important thing is to heat the butter until it's almost—but not quite—burned, and to cook the pasta perfectly al dente. If you can find fresh or frozen pasta sheets, feel free to use those instead of making your own.

SERVES 4 TO 6

Pasta
3 CUPS UNBLEACHED ALL-PURPOSE FLOUR,
    PLUS ADDITIONAL FOR DUSTING
4 LARGE EGGS, LIGHTLY BEATEN
1 TEASPOON FINE SALT

Filling
1 CUP FROZEN PEAS
1 CUP ROASTED ALMONDS
8 OUNCES GOAT CHEESE

Brown Butter Sauce
½ CUP (1 STICK) BUTTER
1 SHALLOT (ABOUT 1 TABLESPOON), DICED

(continued next page)

Make the pasta: In a food processor, blend the flour, eggs, salt, and 2 tablespoons of water for 2 minutes, or until the mixture just begins to form a ball. If the dough crumbles to the touch, continue processing while slowly adding 1 more tablespoon of water. The dough must be firm but not sticky. Remove from the machine and transfer to a floured surface, then knead by hand for 10 minutes. Cover loosely with a plastic wrap and let sit for 1 hour so that the gluten relaxes.

To roll the pasta, divide the dough into 8 pieces, then cover them loosely with plastic wrap. Set the rollers of a pasta machine on its widest setting. Take one piece of dough and roll out into a long rectangle to feed through the machine, about ¼-inch-thick and 2 inches wide. Lightly dust it with flour, and feed through the rollers. Fold the pasta sheet in half and feed it, folded end first, through the machine again. Repeat 7 more times, dusting with flour when necessary, and turning the machine's dial to a narrower setting each time.

The resulting sheet of pasta will be paper-thin, and about 4 inches wide by 36 inches long. Lay out to dry for about 10 minutes. The traditional Italian method is to drape pasta sheets over chairs and counters: do what works. Repeat with the next 7 pieces of dough.

Make the filling: Add the peas, almonds, and goat cheese to the work bowl of a food processor and pulse until the mixture is smooth. Transfer to a mixing bowl.

To assemble the ravioli: Lay out a sheet of pasta and cut it into 4-inch squares. Arrange the pasta squares on a floured work surface. Place 3 teaspoons of the ravioli filling into the center of each square. Place another square on top, and seal the edges together by pressing down firmly with the tines of a fork. When all of the ravioli have been formed, cover them loosely with a clean, lightly floured kitchen towel.

To cook the pasta: Add ¼ cup of salt to a large stockpot of water over high heat and bring to a boil.

While waiting for the water to come to a boil, add the butter and shallot to a medium saucepan over medium-high heat. When the butter starts to bubble, give the pan a quick swirl, and continue cooking for about 4 minutes, or until the shallots are golden-brown and the butter solids have turned dark brown. Remove from the heat, cover, and keep warm.

Cook the ravioli in small batches (about 8 squares per batch). Boil each batch for about 4 minutes, or as long as it takes for the ravioli to float to the surface, and then 1 minute longer. As the batches finish cooking, toss with a bit of the butter sauce in a large serving bowl. Incorporate thoroughly and serve.

Rack of Lamb with Cucumber Aspic

Although cucumber aspic may strike some as odd, it adds a delightful freshness to the gamey flavors of the lamb. Feel free to experiment with other flavors after mastering the trick of making aspic. You will need to marinate the lamb overnight, so plan ahead.

SERVES 4 TO 6

1 CUCUMBER, ROUGHLY CHOPPED

1 BUNCH ITALIAN PARSLEY, STEMS REMOVED AND ROUGHLY CHOPPED

1½ TEASPOONS FINE SALT, DIVIDED

2 TABLESPOONS EXTRA-VIRGIN OLIVE OIL

2 GARLIC CLOVES (ABOUT 2 TABLESPOONS), THINLY SLICED

1 SPRIG FRESH ROSEMARY

1 FULL RACK OF LAMB (ABOUT 1 POUND), CUT INTO TWO SECTIONS

½ PACKET (ABOUT ½ TEASPOON) UNFLAVORED GELATIN

The day before you plan to serve the lamb, combine the cucumber, the parsley, and a teaspoon of salt in the work bowl of a food processor. Purée the mixture, and transfer it to a fine-mesh strainer set over a larger mixing bowl. Allow the mixture to drain in the refrigerator overnight. This process should yield about one cup of cucumber juice after discarding the solids.

Prepare the lamb marinade a day in advance as well. Combine the oil, garlic, rosemary, and the remaining half teaspoon of salt in a sealable container large enough to accommodate the lamb. Coat the lamb with this mixture, making sure to rub it into and under the lamb's layer of fat. Seal the container, transfer it to the refrigerator, and marinate the lamb overnight.

The day you plan to serve the dish, slowly mix the gelatin with a quarter cup of the cucumber juice until it starts to thicken and the gelatin dissolves, about 2 minutes. In a small saucepan over medium-low heat, heat up the remaining cucumber juice, making sure it does not boil. As soon as the juice is hot to the touch, turn off the heat, and whisk it slowly into the gelatin mixture. Pour the combined mixture into a square glass or ceramic container, about ½-inch deep, and refrigerate at least 1 hour.

Preheat the oven to 350°F. Set a large oven-safe sauté pan over medium-high heat. Place both pieces of the lamb, fat layer down, in the pan and sear until it turns crispy and brown, about 8 minutes. Flip the lamb over, and transfer it to the oven. Cook for 5 minutes, or until an instant-read thermometer registers 130°F (for medium-rare). Remove the lamb from the oven and let it rest for 4 minutes.

While the lamb rests, take the aspic out of the refrigerator, unmold it, and slice it into 2-inch-thick squares. Slice the lamb between the rib bones so the pieces look like little meat lollipops. Fan the lamb pieces out and place one square of cucumber aspic on top of each just before serving.

Chocolate and Salt Torte

This classic is modernized with the addition of salt. It's a small change, but essential: generally desserts are less sweet, or embrace a more complex sweetness, than they did in the fifties and sixties. The kosher salt here takes the rich bitterness of chocolate to the center stage.

SERVES 4 TO 6

1 CUP (8 OUNCES) SEMISWEET CHOCOLATE PIECES

2 STICKS (1 CUP) UNSALTED BUTTER

1 CUP GRANULATED SUGAR

1 CUP UNSWEETENED COCOA POWDER

6 MEDIUM EGGS

1½ TABLESPOONS KOSHER SALT

Preheat the oven to 375°F. Spray a 9-inch springform pan with nonstick cooking spray, then line the bottom with a circle of parchment paper. Spray the paper with cooking spray, then set the pan aside.

Place the chocolate and butter in a double boiler over medium-low heat, or set in a heatproof mixing bowl over a pan of simmering water, being careful not to let the bowl touch the water. Stirring often, melt the chocolate with the butter until it is completely blended. Remove from the heat and transfer the chocolate-butter mixture to a large mixing bowl. Add the sugar and cocoa, and mix well with a whisk or an electric mixer. Add the eggs one at a time, whisking well after each addition. Sprinkle the salt evenly on the bottom of the prepared springform pan, then slowly pour the batter into the prepared pan.

Place the pan on the top rack of the oven and bake for 30 minutes, or until the cake has risen and its top has formed a thin crust. The cake should be firm in the center when done.

Cool for 10 minutes, then invert onto a plate, removing the sides of the springform pan. Remove and discard the parchment paper and set the cake aside to cool completely, about 35 minutes.

BEVERAGE PAIRINGS

With the endive salad, either a Pinot Gris from Alsace or a Gewürztraminer from Germany are the top choices. Both will modulate the double whammy of blue cheese and endive with just a hint of sweetness. Stay away from reds or bone-dry white wines or else the dish will become unbearably bitter. For a beer pairing, a Belgian abbey ale is the way to go. Its sweet and spicy character adds a near-perfect balance to the salad.

Since the ravioli and the lamb should be served together, we will have one pairing suggestion for both of them. With this dish, you should consider a Premier Cru Burgundy from the Gevrey Chambertin district. However, if you (like I do) blanch at spending $100 on a single bottle of wine, there is another option: a Pinot Noir from the Santa Maria Valley in Santa Barbara has a similar flavor profile. Beer is not a good choice for this dish, at all. It really requires the structure of wine to complement the complexity of its bright and savory notes.

This dessert is one of few that really can work well with wine. This is due to the addition of salt, which moderates the chocolate's sweetness. A late-harvest red Zinfandel from California is a perfect wine match, adding syrupy flavors of blackberries and caramel to the mix. For beer, I choose to pour an imperial stout. Its rich malty notes make the chocolate pop into the stratosphere.

FARMERS' MARKET FEAST

There is a secret that chefs keep from you. It's also the very thing you probably never wanted to hear (especially after buying the latest cookbook). Trust me, knowing the secret will change how you think about food and cooking forever. Here it is: There is no such thing as a perfect recipe. Unless you happen to live in a parallel universe made entirely of Legos, every fruit and vegetable is unique. This truth is at its most obvious at the farmers' market, where vegetables look like nature intended.

On your next trip, take a look at the tomatoes. Each is a different size, shape, and shade. When you cut them open, the differences literally squirt out: each has its own unique ratio of flesh and juice. Each bite you take will have a slightly different proportion of sweet and sour. So when a recipe calls for a tomato, what does that mean? It means you are free to experiment: the best way to make a great meal is to improvise. Once you have made a recipe once or twice, you can take as many detours as you like. Of course cookbook recipes need precise measurements, but that's not how I really cook. I don't measure perfect teaspoons of salt: I have fun! The recipes in this chapter are all begging you to tweak them and make them your own. You have my permission. Take the time to appreciate the differences in each piece of food you purchase, think about what will bring its flavor profile to the next level, and then have a good time.

Cucumber Salad with Marcona Almonds

Keep the goat cheese in the refrigerator until the last minute so that it will crumble over the salad rather than melt in your fingers. Also, don't try to make this dish at any time other than during the spring: garlic scapes won't be available. The other key element of this dish is cutting the cucumbers into precise tiny sticks, a knife technique called batonnet.

SERVES 4 TO 6

2 TABLESPOONS EXTRA-VIRGIN OLIVE OIL

¼ CUP MARCONA ALMONDS (OR ROASTED, SALTED ALMONDS)

1 GARLIC SCAPE, ROUGHLY CHOPPED

1½ CUPS OF YOUR FAVORITE SALAD GREENS (WATERCRESS IS AN
    EXCELLENT CHOICE), RIPPED INTO BITE-SIZED PIECES

1 SMALL CUCUMBER, CUT INTO BATONNET (½-INCH X ½-INCH X
    3-INCH PIECES)

½ TEASPOON FINE SALT

3 TABLESPOONS FRESH GOAT CHEESE

1 SMALL NAVEL ORANGE, CUT INTO WEDGES

In a small sauté pan over medium-high heat, heat the olive oil. Add the almonds and the garlic scape, and sauté for 5 minutes, or until the scape starts to brown. Remove from heat, discard the scape, reserve the almonds and oil, and let them cool for 10 minutes.

Place the salad greens, cucumbers, and the reserved almonds and oil in a large mixing bowl and toss to combine. Sprinkle the salt on top and toss once more.

Place the salad on a large serving plate. Generously crumble the goat cheese on top. Arrange the orange wedges around the salad for an eye-catching presentation, and serve.

Fava Beans with Mint and Bacon

Fava beans are a springtime treat and well worth a bit of manual labor. Look for pods that are firm and bright green, with as little browning as possible. It will take at least one half hour to shell these beans. The resulting dish is a bit soupy, so serving with a hunk of French bread is a great touch.

SERVES 4 TO 6

1 TABLESPOON EXTRA-VIRGIN OLIVE OIL

½ TABLESPOON UNSALTED BUTTER

5 BACON SLICES (ABOUT 5 OUNCES), DICED

2 SPRING ONIONS (OR SCALLIONS), WHITE AND GREEN PARTS
   SEPARATED, MINCED

¾ CUP DRY WHITE WINE

2 CUPS SHUCKED FRESH FAVA BEANS (ABOUT 2 POUNDS OF PODS)

10 FRESH MINT LEAVES

Add the olive oil and butter to a sauté pan over medium-high heat. Melt the butter, and then add the bacon and sauté for 5 minutes, or until the bacon starts to turn brown and crispy. Add the onions and cook until translucent, about 2 to 3 minutes. Add the wine and bring the mixture to a boil, making sure to scrape the bottom of the pan and free up any of those tasty bacon bits. Add 1½ cups of water, bring to a boil, and cook until the mixture is reduced by half.

Lower the heat to a simmer and add the fava beans. Cook for about 5 minutes, until the beans are tender. Add the mint leaves and turn off the heat. Let stand for 4 minutes before serving in individual bowls.

Bread and Tomatoes with Olive Oil

Great quality ingredients will make this, a classic dish of northern Spain, one of the most memorable of your life. The bread should be flaky and firm, the tomatoes perfectly ripe, and the olive oil should be Spanish, preferably from the Catalan region of Northern Spain. Unfortunately, the opposite is true, too: if you use typical supermarket ingredients, this dish will turn out tragically.

SERVES 4

1 FRESH BAGUETTE

2 TOMATOES, HALVED

¼ CUP SPANISH EXTRA-VIRGIN OLIVE OIL

1 TEASPOON KOSHER SALT

Slice the baguette lengthwise, and then in half, yielding four equally-sized pieces of bread. Evenly squeeze the juice and pulp of the tomato onto one of the pieces of bread: The entire top of the bread should be red from the tomato (and the tomato should be reduced to nothing more than a bit of skin to be discarded). Drizzle a tablespoon of olive oil over the top, along with a sprinkling of the salt. Repeat for all four slices. Serve immediately.

Strawberries with Sour Cream and Brown Sugar

This is the favorite dish of my childhood, which is not surprising since I pretty much grew up on porridge and canned peas. The important thing is to use the freshest strawberries you can find, making sure they are not bruised in any way. This dish demonstrates to perfection how ridiculously easy using farm-fresh ingredients in recipes can be!

SERVES 4 TO 6

1 PINT STRAWBERRIES, WITH STEMS
½ CUP SOUR CREAM
½ CUP LIGHT BROWN SUGAR

Put the ingredients in separate bowls, and let your guests do the rest: grab hold of a strawberry by the stem, dip it into the sour cream, and then into the brown sugar. Yep, I told you it was easy!

BEVERAGE PAIRINGS

With the watercress salad, a Muscadet-Sèvre et Maine will accent the almonds and mellow out the goat cheese. A Belgian sour ale or a Basque cider are two other great choices; both will add a bit of zing to this green salad.

For the fava beans, the best beer and wine selections come from France. Either a bière de garde from Flanders or a white wine from Savoie will put this dish over the edge. The beer's fruitiness and dark malty notes isolate the mint and pork flavors in a magical way. The wine pushes the fava bean flavors into the forefront, cutting a diamond out of the simple legume.

With the tomato bread, a Basque cider, a Spanish cerveza especial, or a Cava from Spain will do the trick. Both the cerveza and the cider slice through the olive oil and let loose its core flavors of wild grass and ocean breeze. The Cava accents the bread's crust and provides a smoky minerality to the entire dish.

For the strawberries, a Moscato d'Asti or a strawberry ale are the top choices. The sweetness and barely-there bubbles of the Moscato turn to cream while eating strawberries. The ale puts the strawberries into overdrive and launches them over the moon.

SOURCES

INGREDIENTS

PENZEY'S SPICES

8528 Germantown Ave
Philadelphia, PA 19176
(215) 247-0770
www.penzeys.com
Great for Szechuan peppercorns, dried herbs,
    smoked paprika, vanilla beans, and chiles.

H MART

7052 Terminal Square
Upper Darby, PA 19082
(610) 734-1001
www.hmart.com
Go here for sesame oil, aged soy sauce, cilantro,
    lemongrass, soy products, and coconut milk.

CHEESES

DI BRUNO BROTHERS

930 S. 9th Street
Philadelphia, PA 19147
(215) 922-2876
www.dibruno.com
They're known for their fresh mozzarella, truffle
    oil, walnut oil, chestnut honey, and aged bal-
    samic vinegar.

COWGIRL CREAMERY

919 F Street NW
Washington, D.C. 20004
(202) 393-6880
www.cowgirlcreamery.com
Amazing goat cheeses, boucheron, and Gruyère.

CHERRY GROVE FARM

3200 Lawrenceville Road (Rte. 206)
Lawrenceville, New Jersey 08648
(609) 219-0053
www.cherrygrovefarm.com
Specializing in raw milk cheeses.

PRODUCE

AMISH FARM STAND

Rittenhouse Square Farmers' Market
18th and Walnut Streets
Philadelphia, PA 19103
www.farmtocity.org
Wares include fresh eggs and produce, includ-
    ing garlic scapes, fava beans, artichokes, and
    squashes.

LOCAL HARVEST

www.localharvest.org
    A great way to find nearby farmer's markets

SEAFOOD

SAMUELS & SON SEAFOOD CO.

3407 S. Lawrence Street
Philadelphia, PA 19148
(800) 580-5810
www.samuelsandsonseafood.com
Their specialties are calamari, scallops, and
    shrimp, among many other things.

PIKE'S PLACE FISH

86 Pike Place
Seattle, WA 98101
(800) 542-7732
www.pikeplacefish.com
You can always find fresh calamari, scallops,
    and oysters here with an abundance of other
    choices.

MEATS

AYRSHIRE FARMS

1 East Washington Street
    Middleburg, VA 20117
(540) 592-3689
www.ayrshirefarm.com
You'll find heritage-bred beef, certified organic
    turkey, and humanely-raised pork available
    here.

HEARST RANCH

5 Third Street, Suite 200
San Francisco, CA 94103
(866) 547-2624
www.hearstranch.com
Go here for grass-fed and grass-finished beef
    and lamb.

WINE

WINE LIBRARY

586 Morris Avenue
Springfield, NJ 07081
888-980-WINE (9463)
www.winelibrary.com
There's great pricing and excellent selection of
    wines.

K&L WINE MERCHANTS

3005 El Camino Real
Redwood City, CA 94061
877-KLWines (877-559-4637)
www.klwines.com
Always an extensive selection of collectible
    wines.

BEER

BREWFORIA

3030 E. Overland Road
Meridian ID, 83642
(888) 334-BEER
www.brewforia.com
Nice selection of craft brews from the West Coast.

JOHNS GROCERY.

401 E. Market Street
Iowa City, IA 52245
(319) 337-2183
www.johnsgrocery.com
Excellent selection of international brews.

SPIRITS

ASTOR WINE & SPIRITS

399 Lafayette Street
New York, NY 10003
(212) 674-7500
www.astorwines.com
A well-curated selection of spirits.

EDUCATION

THE WINE SCHOOL OF PHILADELPHIA

127 S.22nd Street
Philadelphia, PA 19103
(215) 965-1514
www.wineschool.us

Keith's school offers Corked & Forked classes.

INDEX